TREE
WISDOM

TREE WISDOM

A YEAR OF HEALING
AMONG THE TREES

VINCENT KARCHE

HAY HOUSE

Carlsbad, California • New York City
London • Sydney • New Delhi

Published in the United Kingdom by:
Hay House UK Ltd, The Sixth Floor, Watson House,
54 Baker Street, London W1U 7BU
Tel: +44 (0)20 3927 7290; Fax: +44 (0)20 3927 7291; www.hayhouse.co.uk

Published in the United States of America by:
Hay House Inc., PO Box 5100, Carlsbad, CA 92018-5100
Tel: (1) 760 431 7695 or (800) 654 5126
Fax: (1) 760 431 6948 or (800) 650 5115; www.hayhouse.com

Published in Australia by:
Hay House Australia Ltd, 18/36 Ralph St, Alexandria NSW 2015
Tel: (61) 2 9669 4299; Fax: (61) 2 9669 4144; www.hayhouse.com.au

Published in India by:
Hay House Publishers India, Muskaan Complex,
Plot No.3, B-2, Vasant Kunj, New Delhi 110 070
Tel: (91) 11 4176 1620; Fax: (91) 11 4176 1630; www.hayhouse.co.in

First published by Leduc.s Éditions, Paris, 2017

Text © Vincent Karche, 2017
Editorial guidance: Pascale Senk
English language translation by Corinne McKay, 2019

A catalogue record for this book is available from the British Library.

Tradepaper ISBN: 978-1-4019-6339-2
E-book ISBN: 978-1-78817-395-7
Audiobook ISBN: 978-1-78817-436-7

Interior images: 1, 53, 99, 143 123RF/paprika; all other illustrations © Claire Nicolet

Printed in the United States of America

To my sister Isabelle.

Everything ends and begins with love…

CONTENTS

PREFACE

Trees are just like us. They are born. They breathe. They grow up. They long for harmony and balance. They grow to their full potential. They die.

Like brothers and sisters who are always available, trees are always there for you. If you dare to accept their generous offer, a clear and endless horizon will open up for you: when you get close to a tree, you will understand how you support each other. You will feel siblinghood; the simple joy of living and breathing together. You will feel at peace in any situation. Trees do all of this so naturally.

Dare to touch a tree. Dare to smell it, to press your heart against it. Embrace a tree and your emotions will come back to you a hundredfold. Trees have a zest for life that will expand to welcome you just as you are.

At difficult moments, trees can inspire you. They can help to heal your wounds and bring you peace. In the warm embrace of their branches, you are born again. And sometimes trees are still there for you, even though they are a long way away.

As time goes by, like a tree you will love growing old and passing on your wisdom, and you will grow to appreciate your times of effort and ease.

For now, it is important for you to check in with every statement in this book. This is not a book about religion. It is the result of observing and exchanging; of a life that has been lived. Live your own life: walk through woods and forests, observe, feel, make every wisdom your own and make a note of your perceptions when you return from your walks. If you wish, write your thoughts in a special notebook or journal.

A solitary tree and a tree in a city park both have much to teach us, but when it comes to the message of this book, seeing your life as part of a forest will be particularly inspiring, leading you to be more comfortable in your relationships with yourself and others.

In temperate countries, trees live according to the rhythms of the four seasons of the year. So it seemed right to me to align the 12 tree wisdoms with the 12 months of the year, especially as the four seasons of the year match the four seasons of our lives: sprouting, blossoming, transforming and resting peacefully.

To help you truly experience tree wisdom, I have some exercises to offer you. These are easy to do. They are inspired by more than 25 years of exploration: breathing techniques learned from great singing masters; fasciatherapy seminars; meditation retreats at the Kopan Buddhist temple in Kathmandu, Nepal; the intense silences of the Benedictine monastery of Saint-Benôit-du-Lac, Quebec; learning to be present at the First Nation cultural site of Tsonontwan, Quebec; and years of psychotherapy, in various forms. All of these experiences have nurtured what I offer you here.

Finally, along with each wisdom, I offer you a short poem and invite you to write a poem of your own. Let a poem, a slam, a haiku, a song or even a single word spring forth.

Be assured that this book is just as much yours as it is mine. Make it your own. Live it, with all of your senses.

Trees love you. Let them join you on an exploration of who you are.

Welcome to this journey, in the company of the great masters.

TREES, MY BIG BROTHERS AND SISTERS

Tree. When I meet you or I hear about you, I feel a deep wave of gratitude. Because I've spent time with you and become entwined with your destiny, I've learned about the incredible gifts you've given the world. I feel grateful for them right this moment. You give life. You love life. You are life. I owe you nothing. I feel like a son who sometimes wanders away, but who comes back to you to find some comfort. Tree, my big brother, you're always there for me – when I'm happy, when I'm hurting, when I'm angry, or just for no reason at all. In my quiet, empty moments, you inspire me.

My first job was working in the woods – a logical continuation of my childhood in northeastern France's heavily wooded

Lorraine region. I remember the forest in Moyeuvre, near where I grew up, and the forest in the Vosges region of eastern France, where I went on summer holidays with my family. These forests were where I felt close to my father, a true nature lover. Trees were one of the few, precious, things we had in common.

I was a bit ignorant and idealistic when I was younger. I travelled the world and was surprised to find that humans sometimes cut trees down by the hundreds, or dug them up to see how they would grow if they were moved to a different location. I learned that the most valued trees were the strongest, the straightest and the most beautiful, and that those were stuffed full of chemicals and given space to grow through selective thinning of the forest around them.[1] Tough luck for the other trees, those that were considered weak, ugly or useless for logging, only good for paper or wood shavings. They were left to fend for themselves.

I saw huge clear-cuts, swathes of the Earth made sterile, made into deserts that would endure for decades. I asked myself how

---

1 In forestry, selective thinning is done to promote the growth of some trees by culling those that are seen as weaker or of lower quality. At the end of the forest life cycle, thinning allows more light to enter the forest to help the young trees to regenerate the forest.

many logging executives saw trees simply as gold ingots made of wood...

Faced with these mercenary policies, I felt sick; I cried when I thought about them. I had only one desire, trees: to reconnect with you, with the feelings I'd had for you for a long time, and to make sure those brutal practices had nothing to do with you. I decided to pursue a different kind of career, protecting, preserving and respecting you. I met new people: directors of nature reserves, estate managers, conservationists who managed forests almost exactly as nature would have done. People who observed you simply for the joy of discovering how you lived, who you were.

And then, in 1991, my life was turned upside down. I was 23 years old and I was doing forest research in Burundi, in central Africa, for my French national service. This was a thrilling experience that provided much-needed wood for the people of Burundi, a charming country known as 'the land of 1,000 hills'. We had to choose − from a few varieties of Central American pine and Australian eucalyptus − the trees that would grow best there. That's how I learned about *Pinus patula, Eucalyptus globulus* and *Pinus maximinoi*, among others.

Decades-long tests had already been done around the world, and I was there to gather the results from the stands of trees that my predecessors had planted. Of course the goal was to increase the forests' productivity, but also to increase the forest cover and improve the living conditions of the people of Burundi – one of the world's poorest countries. It wasn't a perfect model, but it made sense.

My stay in Burundi gave me another gift: singing. It was a childhood passion of mine and I joined a choir in Bujumbura to pass the time in the evenings. Nothing unusual in that, until the choir director exclaimed, after hearing me sing, 'You have the potential to become a world-class operatic tenor.' At the time, I had no idea what that meant, or where it would lead me.

Two years later, I was back in France. I had been hired as a forestry technician in the beautiful southwestern city of Carcassonne and was responsible for the forests in the surrounding area. At the same time, I started studying classical singing near Toulouse.

Along with preventing forest fires in the towns near the Mediterranean, I had to produce or sell wood on private land, where profitability expectations ran high.

A year of that was enough to convince me to attempt the impossible: leaving my job to become a professional singer. But it wasn't impossible. After training for several years in Montpellier, Nice and then Strasbourg, I launched my career as an international tenor, along with the thrilling highs and crushing lows of the life of an opera star.

Every time that I had to take on a new role – Werther in Massenet's *Werther*, Tamino in Mozart's *The Magic Flute*, Fenton in Verdi's *Falstaff*, or Orpheus in Offenbach's *Orpheus in the Underworld* – I would go and find a tree, either in a forest or a city park, so that it could hold my hand before I went on stage.

It wasn't enough. In 2003, under ever-increasing pressure and feeling less and less at home under the lights and in the false, claustrophobic atmosphere of the theatre, I lost my voice and my will to live. But what seemed like a disaster – the end of my high-flying career – finally allowed me to find myself by finding you again, trees.

Here's what happened: I was physically and emotionally exhausted and running out of money, and I went to visit a

First Nations chief in Quebec, Canada. That was my refuge.[2] I was supposed to stay for a few days, but the trip turned into a four-month immersion initiation.

The chief of the Huron-Wendat First Nation helped me get back to basics. By 'basics', I mean the essence of things. When I arrived, it was minus 15° Celsius, and the chief's first words to me were, 'Observe nature. Watch the trees. Every lesson is there.' Thanks to him, and to a half-dog, half-wolf, and to the trees in Quebec, I learned how to live again. No thoughts, no regrets and no concerns about the future. Just living.

Trees … you must understand how grateful I am to you. In Quebec, I saw you again, touched you, smelled you, felt you. From you, I learned how to live. I discovered your boundless and unconditional gifts. I breathed in the silence of your hollows, pressed against your trunks. I caught glimpses of the ancient world that lives on in your memories. Five hundred years, 2,000 years, even 10,000 years – you live an inconceivable amount of time compared to a human life. How could I not bow before you?

2　I discuss this in detail in my book *Un loup dans la gorge: L'homme qui avait perdu sa voix puis retrouvé son âme* (A Wolf in the Throat: The man who lost his voice and found his soul). Favre, 2015.

Later on, when my confidence and creativity returned, the facts of the situation struck me. When I sang, I missed your presence. And when I was in a forest, I felt like singing. So, in 2011, I created a new career for myself: as a tenor singer and forest guide, through my project RandOlyric.[3] This career allows me to combine my two passions and share them with others, both adults and children. Together, we feel alive and we sing. With you, trees.

Ah, trees, all the years I worked in forestry, you whispered to me through your leaves. You whispered when I was reborn in the forests of Quebec and when I spent countless hours meditating at your feet. You're whispering to me now, during RandOlyric walks. And now I understand. When I am with you, I am with myself.

And everything you've given me is set down here, in the 12 wisdoms that I'm going to share in this book.

Trees, thank you. I love you.

---

3   RandOlyric offers sensory immersion walks during which we explore our voices in a powerful natural environment. The trees inspire us to sing together, either opera or improvised songs.

SPRING

A Time of Awakening

It's springtime. Sweetness and softness have returned to the Earth. Buds are drawing on energy deep within and unfolding, slowly and timidly at first, and then, once they're sure that the winter's chill has gone for good, exploding with all their might. Every flower, leaf and branch is stretching out as far as it possibly can, reaching out for the sun's pure joyful warmth.

In the forest, everything is singing. Choirs of birds are offering their most beautiful melodies to the trees, and the trees are echoing them back from their bark, whether rough or smooth. Delicate green leaves are rustling at the slightest breath of air, brushing against each other and caressing the sky in a cascading chorus.

Boundless energy is bubbling up from deep within the earth. Nothing is holding back; there is abundance everywhere – completely natural, and completely shared.

As spring dawns, the trees sound the call: for openness, sharing and abundance.

BREATHE

Breathing is the most natural action in the world, and also the most shared. Every living thing on Earth breathes, but we don't all breathe in the same way. Breath is a bridge between the internal and the external; the quality of our relationship with ourselves and with other living things depends on **the quality of our breath**.

Trees teach us about breathing. They continually produce oxygen, so they teach us about rejuvenation and about our perception of ourselves. They help us to feel stronger, while remaining peaceful.

The Breath of Trees

We don't see trees breathing and we don't hear them breathing either, but science tells us that they do breathe. Like humans,

trees must keep breathing in order to live. As humans, we find our breath comes and goes without thought or effort on our part; but if we stop breathing for even a short time, we die. Trees are a little different: if we cut all of the leaves and branches off a tree in the middle of its growing season, reducing its breathing considerably, its growth will slow down, but it will find the strength within itself to come back to life (*see the Eighth Wisdom*).

Trees are great **transformers of waste**. For this waste-processing system to work, though, there can't be too much pollution in the air. When we emit greenhouse gases and industrial pollution and cut down trees, are we aware of the damage we're doing?

✂ HOW TREES BREATHE ✂

Trees breathe in two ways. First, they can breathe exactly as humans do: by taking in oxygen and releasing carbon dioxide. Every cell in a tree does this, in winter and in summer. This metabolic process – using oxygen to burn sugars – gives the tree the energy its cells need to multiply and grow.

Trees also breathe through photosynthesis: in late spring and throughout the summer, their leaves or needles work symbiotically with sunlight to absorb carbon dioxide and produce oxygen. Evergreen trees – fir, scrub oak, etc. – can keep photosynthesis going in the winter to a lesser degree, as long as the weather isn't below freezing, or at least not for very long. Photosynthesis creates a chemical reaction within each leaf or needle and that in turn produces the organic material that the tree needs in order to grow.

The Moyeuvre Forest

I took my first breaths in the maternity ward in Moyeuvre-Grande, a small steel-mill city in Lorraine. At that time, if you had passed through Moyeuvre-Grande without paying too much attention to your surroundings, you might have noticed nothing more than factory chimneys spewing black smoke, tailings heaps dotted across limestone hills, kilometres of pipelines, and lines of freight wagons that barely concealed the eruptions taking place inside them. Most important of all, you would have **breathed air that was not fit to be breathed**. And a cloud of sulphur would have settled on your skin and clothes.

But if you had looked beyond the hustle and bustle of the steel mill, you would have seen a vast forest running up the hillsides – a beech forest, one of the most beautiful in France, my father always said. Later on, one of the forest wardens told me the same thing. The beech trees were fast-growing; they had straight, strong trunks and symmetrical rings. The wood they produced was exceptional in quality. They were used to make furniture and flooring, and sometimes even slivered into wood veneer. **Humans are driven by this kind of compulsion – always thinking about market value**.

I thought that every one of those trees was beautiful – even the ones that were twisted or split in two. I thought the hornbeams were beautiful. The forest wardens called them 'unremarkable understorey trees' and considered them only good for firewood. But they served another purpose: supporting the soaring trunks of the larger beech while blocking the light and preventing the lower branches from growing. This promoted 'natural pruning', which is the option of choice for high-value woods.

People call hornbeams 'trees for the blind', because their bark, with its soft vertical striations, is immediately recognizable to the touch. **Even someone who cannot see can recognize a hornbeam.** What a wonderful gift to the world!

My parents lived on the edge of the Moyeuvre forest, and that's where I learned to breathe. There, away from the cares of my daily routine, I found a balm to soothe my childhood worries. There, I could feel the smell of sulphur evaporating and could draw in as much fresh, new air as I wanted. I spent hours in the forest, playing and building forts. I staked out a cave full of fossils, and sometimes I took friends there, or my pet dachshund. But most of the time I went there alone.

I loved being alone, surrounded by trees. I felt connected to the trees, but also to all living things. We were all connected, and here was the proof: **we were all breathing the same air**. Wasn't that incredible?

I felt alone and at the same time at one with the world.

Trees Are Givers

Trees don't just give us fresh air; they give, and give, and give. **Trees reassure us. They protect us. They allow us to play, to escape and to be consciously alone. This helps us connect to ourselves and to other people.**

Have you ever felt surrounded by a life-giving force? Have you ever felt surrounded by brothers and sisters, whose arms, whose branches, were reaching out to welcome you? Have you ever sheltered from a storm or from high winds under a tree's broad crown and felt completely safe and secure? Have you ever felt the coolness of a summer forest protecting you from the blistering sun? Have you ever climbed a tree – a natural staircase to the sky? Have you ever encountered any of the living things that are protected by trees? Trees have so many species living in their embrace; they have lichens on their skin, birds' nests in their armpits, spiders, owls and ants hiding in their nostrils.

And their generosity doesn't end there. People who scan the earth for mushrooms or berries know that the earth depends on organic matter from trees – dead leaves and branches – to regenerate. In the mountains, the thicker this organic layer is, the more the soil is protected from erosion. Trees also saturate the soil with nutrients and it becomes richer and thicker as a result. It also benefits from the 'umbrella' of a tree's branches; this slows the fall of raindrops and keeps trenches from forming on the ground.

There is no end to the list of the benefits we get from trees!

Trees Are Producers

Products, too: furniture, lumber, fuel, flooring, barrels, boats, houses, bridges, sculptures, corks, paper, maple syrup to sweeten the Canadian winters, birch sap for purification… The list goes on and on.

Indigenous peoples have maintained their knowledge of trees' medicinal properties. There was cedar bark mixed into the Labrador tea[4] that the Huron-Wendat chief gave me to cure my inability to be present.

Trees also offer us the **many benefits of their essential oils**. Some, like pine, eucalyptus and cedar, help us to breathe. And what would our modern world be without petroleum, which is produced in part through the decomposition of trees?

Trees Absorb Our Pain

The forests of Alsace and Lorraine, in northeastern France, offer examples of another gift that trees give us. I've walked in every one of these forests, along the Tranchée de la Calonne,

---

4   A drink prepared from the leaves of the Greenland tea bush, which is widespread in North American forests. It is also used to make essential oil.

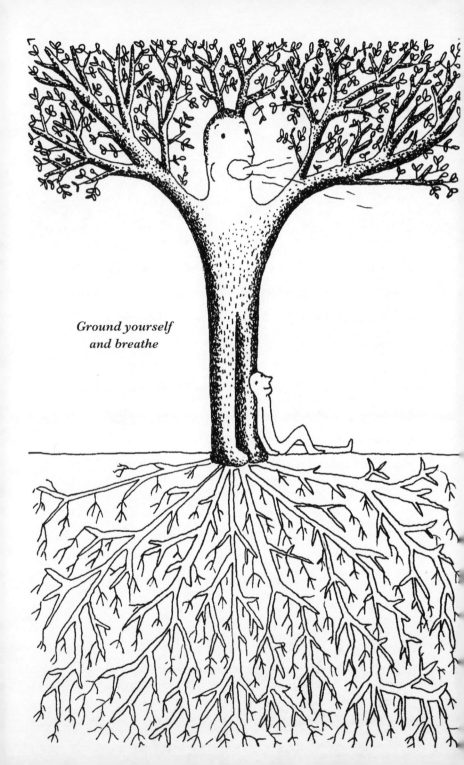

*Ground yourself
and breathe*

near Verdun, and along the crest of the Vosges mountains, in the region that during the two World Wars was both a regional border and France's national border with Germany. I've seen bomb craters and I've seen bullets lodged in tree trunks. These stigmata are still there after 60 or 100 years ... but **these places that were once hell on Earth are now vibrant and peaceful**. The shouts of soldiers and the roar of artillery have been silenced by the leaves of trees. At first the bloody ground was speckled with light green; then, as the years passed, it was submerged by an ocean of darker green. And deep in the earth, to this day, tree roots are embracing rusted bombs, forming a natural shield that prevents them from exploding.

Have you ever tested your ability to silence the cries of your internal conflicts? Have you ever screamed in the woods on a windy day? Have you ever freed yourself from obsessive thoughts by caressing a tree trunk 20 times taller than you? Go on. I dare you.

Trees don't judge. They accept you as you are.

Epilogue: The Beauty of Give-and-Take

Trees provide us with so much love, and that love has its roots in the communion between earth and sky. These offer up everything that trees need to nurture us – water, light, minerals and organic nutrients. So, trees teach us that **the act of giving is intertwined with the act of receiving**, without expectation. All of this just *is*.

Why not use this wisdom as inspiration? Isn't it true that life, like breathing, is a never-ending tide of motion, drawing energy from itself, nourishing itself, pulsating in rhythm, forever? What if we were to see the lack of balance in our lives as a loss of awareness of this wisdom, as a loss of clarity caused by our overactive minds,[5] our fears, inflexible desires, illusory expectations … by all of the constraints that are caused by our original wounds? And what if the answer were simply to reconnect to this wisdom? To relearn this effortless, boundless give-and-take, which is as simple as breathing?

---

5   In my experience, 'overthinking' – too many thoughts spinning too quickly, whether they are positive or negative – prevents us from feeling what is. We identify with our thoughts and emotions rather than with what we are. This keeps us from feeling the fullness of life. This is what meditation practice involves: putting our thoughts in their proper place within the infinite space of what is.

EXERCISE

BREATHE WITH A TREE

When you are out walking in the woods or in a park, choose a tree. It doesn't matter what it's like – it can be large or small, young or old. Just choose the tree you feel most drawn to.

Walk over to the tree. Stand facing it, a few metres away from its trunk, making sure that you can see it from top to bottom.

Greet the tree and ask for permission to do this exercise with it.[6]

Now, without taking your eyes off the tree, anchor yourself in the earth. Place your feet shoulder-width apart, then spread the soles of your feet on the earth. Ground yourself there.

Next, feel your breath entering and leaving your body. Become aware of the interior of your nostrils. Become aware of the coolness of your in-breaths and the warmth of your out-breaths. Notice that your breathing happens effortlessly. Observe it.

---

6   Indigenous peoples respect every living thing, including trees. They find nothing odd in talking to a tree and creating a ritual around their relationship with it. I found this strange at first, but now I take it as a given.

Once this rhythm is established, feel roots growing down from your feet into the earth each time you exhale.

Each time you inhale, feel energy flowing up through your roots and filling your body.

Allow your roots to grow, to expand, to dig more deeply into the earth. Let the tree be your guide. Let the tree's roots touch yours; let them intertwine. Feel them anchoring you more fully with every exhalation. Your roots may go down so deeply that you feel as if you have reached the centre of the Earth.

Be with all of this for a few moments and just feel where you are. Feel the tree. Feel your connection with yourself and with the tree. Feel the connection between earth and sky. Feel the abundance flowing through you.

Let yourself feel this for as long as you want. Then, when you feel you have finished this first exercise, thank the tree by giving it a hug.

Give it a name, too, if you like. My tree's name is Doug, because it's a Douglas fir.

TIME TO CREATE

After your time with the tree, write down what you are feeling. You can do this in the woods or when you get home. While you are writing, connect to the breath flowing through your nostrils, just as you did during the exercise.

~ DOUG ~

There you are, my brother.

Your heart is scarlet. You cry tears of sap.

Your citrus scent wafts to the sky.

You proud and tender giant.

Finally, I take you in my arms.

RESPECT YOUR OWN RHYTHM

'Late', 'early', 'too fast', 'too slow'… At one time or another, who hasn't had the feeling of being inadequate or of life passing them by? Or maybe of wasting time in the middle of a group of people who seem frozen in the face of a situation they can't understand? Who hasn't felt obliged to follow a rhythm dictated by school, by a job, by family or by society? Who hasn't railed against government bureaucracy or a late train?

Trees remind us of something we've forgotten: we don't all move through the world at the same pace. Trees encourage us to have a different perspective on our singularity and to stop comparing ourselves to others. They also remind us to be at peace with our own rhythm.

Wasted Years?

I had to fight to become a forestry worker. And explaining it to my friends and family was even harder. Everyone had given up on me after I'd spent three years at university studying science and left without a degree to show for it. Teachers might have excused my kind of grades and offered extra support at primary, middle and even secondary school, but definitely not at university. There, you're on your own. And I was like an overgrown teenager messing around, not finding my way, just vegetating, a little depressed, not knowing what to do with my life. And here's why: I was barely 17 when I started at university after jumping a year at school. 'He's brilliant but immature,' my teachers said. I was certainly immature.

My parents had thought they were doing the right thing by teaching me to read at the age of three. Early on, they thought that I was fairly gifted, so they pushed me to step things up. The result: I skipped a year and went to primary school early, before I was even five years old. My life was turned upside down. But still my parents were careful: my mother was a teacher at the school, so she was able to keep an eye on me. And then my father took charge of my education for the first two years of middle school.

Skipping a year made my parents proud, and, I'll admit, sometimes me as well, but it became a millstone around my neck when I was 11 or 12: there was just too much of a disconnect between my intellectual maturity and my physical maturity. And I grew more and more distant from my peers; hence my failure at university.

Inside, I felt torn apart. I wasn't interested in anything. **I was a little tree, exposed too soon to the pressure of acting like an adult.** And I paid for it with three empty years – waiting for my maturity to catch up with me, trying to recapture the carefree spirit that I had lost too soon.

At the age of 19, I had to convince my parents that this time I had found my path – a path that would stimulate my senses and unleash my zest for life. I was going to become a forestry technician, and that would make me happy. I also had to convince the instructors at one of the four further education establishments that offer a BTS (a two-year technical degree) in 'forestry production' that I would be a brilliant addition to their programme, despite having done nothing with my life for three years. That wasn't easy, because your academic record follows you for your whole life.

To reassure everyone and show how motivated I was, I decided to do a forestry internship. Seized with a determination that I hadn't felt for a long time, I contacted the directors of the French national forestry office in Sarrebourg, in the Moselle region.

The engineer from the forestry office wrote back right away: 'We are pleased to offer you a one-month internship in the Dabo forest. Contact the forestry technician listed below. He will await your arrival as of 1 May 1987. Yours sincerely, etc…'

I had found my place: the Dabo forest.

Dabo: A Joyful Forest

The Dabo forest, in the Vosges mountains of eastern France, was where I had spent my summers. My grandparents would rent a cottage in the small village of La Hoube, and our whole family would gather there. It was pure joy. I particularly remember our walks, to the soft, gentle rhythm of my grandfather's steps. I remember my grandmother – a sore loser if ever there was one – laughing like crazy when she lost at Scrabble or rummy. The trees brought us together there and I reconnected to my inner sense of joy.

🌿 THE NAMES OF TREES 🌿

A tree's name generally includes a characteristic that allows us to identify it clearly. For example, the silver fir's Latin name, *Abies alba*, reminds us that its bark is a very light whitish-grey. The spruce's Latin name, *Picea abies*, calls to mind its sharp needles and its vague similarity to a fir (*Abies*). The *Picea* are also called *épinette* ('spiky') in Quebec.

The pedunculate oak, *Quercus robur*, reminds us that its acorns are attached to its branches by a long stem, called a peduncle, and its Latin name embodies its strength (*robur*). In North America, the red oak, *Quercus rubra*, shows off its strikingly coloured foliage in its name (red, *rubra*).

The Norway maple, *Acer platanoides*, reminds us that its leaves look like a plane tree's leaves (the Latin name for the plane family is *Platanacae*), while the sugar maple, *Acer saccharum*, makes your mouth water just by its name!

However, everything is relative. In Native American languages, the name for the sugar maple is *Couton* or *Michtan*.

🌿

I arrived in the Dabo forest on a cloudy day, and quickly understood that the forestry technician was not thrilled to have an intern tagging along with him. But he did what he was told. I followed him to all four corners of this **very special spot in the Vosges, ruled by 'the silver king'**: the silver fir. This tree is named for its light grey bark, which sometimes looks almost white. In the Dabo forest, you'll find the silver fir everywhere, from the limestone-filled valleys to the flat-topped mountains, and even on the moist north-facing slopes. There, at an altitude of 500 to 1,000 metres, it is in its element.

It's easy to pick out a silver fir: grab one of its branches firmly with your hand and its needles won't poke you. The needles of the silver fir are flat, and you'll find two rows of white stoma[7] on the underside of each needle. A silver fir's cones face the sky and when they mature, they detach from the tree but don't drop from the branches; they remain where they are. If you find cones at the foot of a tree, or if you see them hanging from the branches, you can be sure that it's not a silver fir.

---

7   These epidermal cells on the inner side of the leaf have many microscopic openings that allow the tree to exchange gases with the atmosphere.

Silver fir are the classic Christmas trees, though the oldest aren't cone-shaped; their upper branches form a plateau. But although the enormous tree in the middle of the main square in Strasbourg commemorates the first mention of a Christmas tree, in the village of Selestat in Alsace, in 1521, you will never see a silver fir in a home today. Because of various factors – mass consumerism, ignorance of how to care for a tree after it's been cut, and the difficulty involved in doing that – many other evergreen trees are passed off as silver fir: Norway spruce, Nordmann fir, Noble fir, Colorado blue spruce and Engelmann spruce, not to mention artificial trees.

Fir Trees: Trees of the Shadows

Not many people know this, but fir trees have a very peculiar characteristic: they love shade. In forestry lingo, we call them 'sciophilous', meaning that they don't like it when the sun hits them all of a sudden. They need time – a lot of time. They need to feel protected for a long time as they're growing – protected by the generations of trees that have come before them. They need years to form a thick, vertical taproot that penetrates deep into the ground; only then do they grow towards the light.

In many places, nature offers these conditions, and forestry workers must learn from nature, regenerating a stand of fir by exposing them to light in a way that is gentle and respectful. It's an art. Because, for the fir tree, aggressive pruning or direct sunlight are even more catastrophic than for other trees.

As part of a team in the Dabo forest, including the forestry technician and a few guards and loggers, I tried this 'light dosing' technique while we were out marking with a hammer the trees that were going to be cut down in the autumn, or during the following winter. Very quickly, I learned the proper technique to cut two ovals out of the bark with the flat side of the hammer, one at chest height and the other on the stump. Later, those marks will show whether the correct tree has been cut down. Then, you use the side of the hammer to put the official government seal on the live wood.

Shade-loving Trees and Sun-loving Trees

In the Dabo forest, we often think of Norway spruce when we think of fir trees. They form what we call a spruce stand.[8] They have short, pointy needles, their bark is reddish-brown

8   In forestry, a stand is a natural spruce forest.

and their cones hang from the branches, falling to the ground when they mature. So, physically, Norway spruce is the exact opposite of silver fir. They also have opposite personalities.

Norway spruce are 'full speed ahead' as soon as they sprout. They grow and grow; they want to race towards the sun as quickly as possible. They aren't that concerned about the depth of their roots; instead, they quickly form shallow, horizontal root systems. Unlike a fir tree's taproot, the roots of Norway spruce are spread out on the surface; you've probably tripped over them when they've erupted through the topsoil on a path. This has an advantage: Norway spruce can thrive in poorer and shallower soil than silver fir can.

Spruce trees love sunshine. Because of that, we call them 'heliophiles'.

Fir trees love sunshine too, but not while they're still growing, because they're patiently creating the conditions to survive once the sun does hit them. **They're putting down deep roots**.

When fir are young, they look fragile and stunted, and may be dwarfed by spruce. But in time they catch up; by the time they're 50 or 100 years old, they're as tall and strong as spruce.

When spruce are young and have their whole lives ahead of them, they're useful to fir because they shade and protect them, while the fir allow the spruce to go up like rockets. It's a beautiful friendship.

Every Tree Has Value

In the forest, every tree has a different personality and no tree is more important than another. Together, they create a harmonious environment in which every tree has its place.

The chief of the Huron-Wendat First Nation told me one day when I was being introduced to his philosophy, 'Here, since the dawn of time there has been a chief guiding the destiny of the various communities.' Then he explained that a chief was not more important than a regular person, a chief simply had an awareness of having been put on this Earth to be a leader. That was totally natural to them and they took great joy in guiding and helping others. Therefore, it made no sense to abuse this power to justify a feeling of superiority, or higher pay. That's a mindset that today's corporate leaders would do well to contemplate.

Each at Its Own Pace

The stand of trees that I hammer-marked in the Dabo forest was on a very steep slope. At the bottom of the slope was a little creek, and the trees there were more robust than those at the top of the slope, because the alluvial sediment enriched the soil. Essentially, those trees were getting an abundance of water and high-quality nutrients, which helped them grow.

Still, **it's not wise to overwhelm young fir trees with chemical fertilizer** or to yank on their upper branches to get them to grow faster. A little fertilizer might give them a short-term energy boost, but there's a risk that it will cause problems later. It's a little like young athletes who take dope, or opera singers who take steroids to salvage a one-night performance. I know something about that.

Launch Time!

After all three public forestry schools rejected my application, I found myself at an interview at the private Poisy-Annecy forestry school. The evaluation of my internship at the Dabo forest was on the table in front of the interviewers. I answered their questions calmly and deliberately. Luckily, they were more concerned with my motivation than with my credentials. I felt welcomed, acknowledged, heard.

Two days later, I learned that I'd been accepted. Once again, the forest had saved me.

Epilogue: Are You a Fir or a Spruce?

What type of tree do you feel more drawn to? To the tree that needs time to grow and hates being the centre of attention? Do you hate talking or singing in front of a class or in public? Are you the type of person who takes a while to mature and who reaches their full potential midway through life, after taking the time to look inwards or perhaps do some psycho-genetic research in order to make peace with your roots and your ancestors? Or are you the type who just forges ahead? Did you attack life from the get-go, without worrying too much about your roots or the future?

Maybe you see yourself in the trees, like hornbeams, who remain in the shadows throughout their lives and are perfectly happy there. Or maybe you drink up the sunshine and only the sunshine, dreading even the slightest wedge of shade, like a Scots pine or a Mediterranean evergreen.

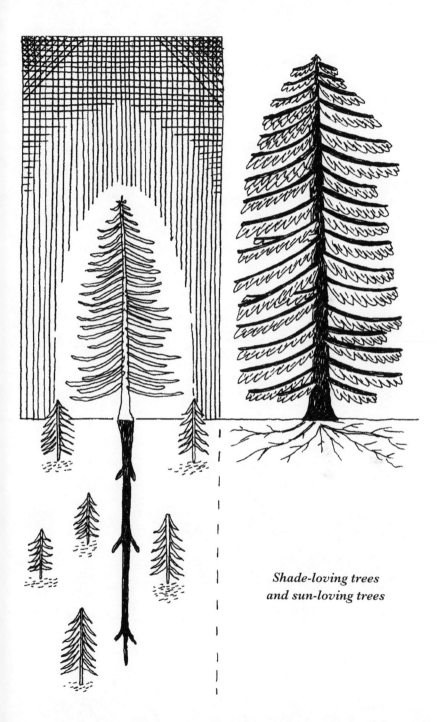

*Shade-loving trees
and sun-loving trees*

Whatever the case, trees show us that these two personality types – spruce and fir – are normal expressions of nature, and of life. **To each their own rhythm. No one is falling behind and no one is getting ahead.** This mindset allows us to relax and stop comparing ourselves to others. If you're a fir and you spend your time wanting to be more like a spruce, you risk driving yourself crazy. Trust me – I did that for a long time.

To be sure, Western society seems to prefer spruce: those who make their mark when they're young; prodigies; young people who are brilliant and dominant, and who know what they want to accomplish before they're 20.

On TV, we see nothing but young athletes, young singers, musicians, actors, entrepreneurs, inventors and personal-growth coaches. You can't get away from them.

So, if you're a spruce, go for it! But if you're more of a fir, now is your chance to learn about patience, to open your mind and to savour the slow and steady progress that will guide you towards the realization of your full potential.

Either way, you will be completely fulfilled if you accept who you are and if you accept your characteristics as normal variations of human existence.

For me, it's clear: I've always been a fir. I love shady undergrowth; I love rain, water, and cloudy days with cleansing storms. Once in a while, I like to experience the desert, or a Mediterranean landscape, but I feel truly at home in a leafy forest where the light enters in slivers and where I feel protected from the wind and freezing temperatures.

Who inspires me? The 'great firs': Nelson Mandela, Gandhi, Sir David Attenborough, or even my friend Marie-Christine, whose zest for life is just coming to fruition at the age of 55. And let's not forget my friend Charles, who has just met the love of his life, aged 65. All of these people are realizing their potential as they reach maturity. Regardless of what they have to give.

EXERCISE

BREATHE WITH YOUR 'TWIN' TREE

Decide for yourself if you are a fir or a spruce. Of course, this is just a general leaning. Things aren't always black or white, and you might behave like a fir in some ways but like a spruce in others. If you're already on the older end of the spectrum, think of the age at which you felt the best, the freest. If you're still young, what is your energy like now? Do you feel totally fulfilled or held back a little?

When you've chosen the type of tree that is most like you, go out and meet one. Take a walk in a park or a forest. Now you'll know how to identify your tree.[9]

Stand about two metres away from your tree and greet it. Ask its permission to do the exercise, as before.

Feel your breath as you face the tree; inhale the cool air and exhale the warm air. Let's call this INEX breathing.

After a while, you will undoubtedly want to have some physical contact with the tree. Take it fully into your arms. Press the trunk of your body against its trunk; press your

---

9   If you can't find any fir or spruce trees near you, here are a few other ideas, listed in ascending order of intensity of characteristics – shade-loving trees: fir, beech, hornbeam; sun-loving trees: oak, spruce, chestnut, Scots pine (and pine trees in general), larch.

heart to its heart; press your forehead or your ear against its bark. Feel the tree, smell the tree, feel its roughness and its density. Feel its strength. Feel your own strength.

Keeping up your INEX breathing, visualize your roots, as you did in the first exercise. If you are a fir, visualize one thick, deep taproot. If you are a spruce, visualize a network of surface roots. Once you've done this, you'll be touching the centre of the Earth if you're a fir tree and you'll be encircling the entire surface of the Earth if you're a spruce. Those are the two ways in which trees anchor themselves.

Stay there for as long as you want. You don't have to stay for very long, but repeat this exercise whenever you can.

When you've finished, thank your tree from the bottom of your heart and give it a name.

TIME TO CREATE

Immediately after meeting your 'twin' tree, go into INEX breathing mode for a few moments and let the words flow from your grateful heart.

~ HELD IN THE SHADOWS ~

Shaded by needles, protected by leaves,
sheltered from the yellow star,

Many young fir trees grow, nestled together,
taking their time.

FEEL CONNECTED TO OTHERS

A forest naturally regulates itself. This is an art – an art of co-existence that develops before our eyes. Anyone who's had the chance to walk through an old-growth forest[10] will recognize it immediately. Trees, plants, moss, fungi, insects and animals all have their place in an ecosystem that is both fragile and miraculous. **The dominant beings are the protectors, while the more fragile provide food and shelter. And one day, the fragile may become the strong.** Plants that are sick or weak die, and become organic matter that strengthens the other living beings. This is also true of

---

10 An old-growth forest or primary forest is a forest that has never been logged or built on by humans. In France, only 0.2 per cent of forest is old-growth forest. Europe's last old-growth forest, the Białowieża forest on the border between Poland and Belarus, is currently threatened with destruction.

prey animals that are eaten by predators. In the soil, mycelium – the vegetative part of a mushroom colony – expands and shores up the connections between tree roots. Each species in the forest makes an irreplaceable contribution to the ecosystem as a whole.

Everything supports and sustains life. This is a major inspiration for us, for we, too, are nature.

The Wormsa Valley

My first RandOlyric walk took place in Alsace, in 2010, in the Wormsa valley. This valley lies below the steep slopes of the Vosges mountains and was hollowed out by a glacier. It's at an altitude of 1,000 metres – an ideal alpine environment.

In the ski station of Gaschney, we took a narrow path – typically used by cows, from the looks of the brown and yellow stains on the grass – to a gentle slope that led us to the small glacial lake of Schiessrothried, some 200 metres below. This lake is penned in by a dam that the Germans built between 1889 and 1894 during the annexation of Alsace-Lorraine,[11] and it's the

---

11 After France was defeated in the war of 1870, Germany took possession of Alsace-Lorraine.

jumping-off point for a trail that leads along the main ridge of the Vosges mountains.

As soon as we crossed the dyke and took the uphill trail on the left, we entered the Wormspel forest, the wild section of the Wormsa valley. The trail looked like a scree slope.[12] Dead trees were piled everywhere. It looked like a giant game of pick up sticks, but there were living trees there too, of all ages and sizes, from the tiniest to the most massive. It bore no resemblance to the beginning of the trail, where the human touch was evident. Here, everything had been left to its own devices. More than one hiker called out: 'They could do some maintenance on the forest, you know!' or, more bluntly, 'This is a big mess!' We're not used to looking at quasi-old-growth forests. Everything has to be organized, sorted, used, then skidded[13] or burned. Clean and clear. Could this be a legacy of the French gardens created for kings? Subconsciously, maybe we feel compelled to tame the wild places...

---

12   A heap of stones or pebbles.
13   In forestry, 'skidding' means transporting logged trees to another location where they are chipped or taken to a processing site.

🌿 WHAT GARDENS TELL US ABOUT 🌿 OUR RELATIONSHIP WITH NATURE

A formal French garden is an organized form of nature; it's laid out carefully and symmetrically. It's immediately recognizable. You can see its ultimate expression in Louis XIV's gardens at Versailles or the Lorraine dukes' gardens at Lunéville. These gardens remind us of an era when the monarch ruled not only people, but nature as well.

At the other end of the spectrum, English gardens, which came later, showed a 'back to nature' preference, and nature wasn't very idealized before the Romantic period. But it was all an illusion: everything was organized by master gardeners. The wild, peaceful spirit of 'real' nature was maintained, but the unpleasant parts were eliminated because man had triumphed over nature. Louis XVI gave Marie-Antoinette an English garden at the Petit Trianon palace; it had an artificial lake, artificial hills and an artificial cave.

English- and French-style gardens both show the human need – at least in the West – to triumph over nature. This egocentric strategy may be rooted in nature's sometimes devastating power. But we must remember what indigenous peoples have never forgotten: that we, too, are nature. We are not separate from it.

Rest assured, no one disturbs the lives of the trees in the Wormsa valley. They sprout, they grow, they die and they rot all on their own. It's a natural glacial cirque. Hands off!

The Healthy Beauty of a Wild Forest

Here's another observation: both of the indicators of good forest health are there in the Wormsa valley. I'm talking about mountain elm and lungwort (*Lobaria pulmonaria*).

In the last decades of the 20th century, elm trees were affected by disease[14] and nearly disappeared from Europe's temperate forests. Since then, the disease has become less virulent and the elm have begun to make a comeback. You have only to meet an elm with broad, lacy, strong, deep green leaves, like those in the Wormspel forest, to see that the place it's living in is thriving.

Now I can see an even rarer lungwort plant right in front of me, clinging to the bark of a tall beech tree, right next to a

---

14 This near-disappearance was caused by a fungal disease – elm disease, also called Dutch elm disease. It's caused by a fungus that's spread by an invasive beetle, the elm bark beetle (*Scolytus scolytus*). There is no cure for it and the affected trees have to be cut down, or, if it's a less severe case, their branches have to be cut off, to avoid spreading the disease to neighbouring trees. The wood is immediately burned.

rivulet running down the hillside. When I was creating my first RandOlyric route, I didn't even see it. A very astute participant pointed it out to us.

Lungwort resembles the branches of the human lung, hence the name. You see it everywhere on the bark of old leafy trees. It's as common as oak or beech, especially in the oldest forests. But it's very sensitive to air pollution and its numbers are declining. As a result, it has been selected as one of the indicators of good health in French forests.

It's often important on our RandOlyric walks. Visually, it's a huge help to those who want to breathe deeply: when you look at a lungwort plant, you can better visualize your lungs filling with air and then emptying, and it helps to know that you're in a completely healthy forest.

The Richness of Diversity

When you walk through a wild forest like Wormspel, you realize that it's doing fine all on its own. You can even find some treasures there, and maybe some wisdom about co-existence.

Elm, maple, fir, spruce, silver birch, ash and beech – the diversity of the Wormspel forest astounds you at every step.

All of these species cling to the hillsides that become steeper as you walk through the forest.

Lower down, near the lake, the giant trees, especially evergreens, rule. As you go higher up, the trunks become slenderer, the crowns shrink back, and the soil gives way to moist, shining rocks. Higher still, the climate is so harsh and the soil so thin that only mountain beech survive – spindly, twisted and not much to look at, but resolutely alive. Finally, above the beech, there is nothing but montane scrub. These are boreal forest conditions; a tree has absolutely no chance of surviving here.

Even though the profusion of species in Wormspel is nothing compared to what you'll find in tropical forests, the abundant contacts between 'community members' is still striking. Because … the trees touch each other. Their leaves touch, their crowns overlap, their trunks intertwine and a blanket of moss and lichen covers them. They are united by the air they breathe and the shadows they cast. And even when they don't touch, their silhouettes reveal that they are still interacting – the dominant ones claiming their space while the followers twist and bend to find slivers of light. Some trees are protectors and others help to hold the space, but all make sure that this three-dimensional mega-organism that we call a forest remains in balance.

Buried or Hidden: An Invisible Support Network

Some things are visible and some are invisible. Beneath a forest lies a web of roots and rootlets, like an internet cable network. **Yes ... the trees talk to each other, they 'write emails' and they exchange substances and information.** If one tree is under attack, or if it is sick, or if it is suffering from a carbon deficit, the rest of the forest is immediately informed, and the influencers put all of their energy into defining a strategy to heal the tree, to allow it to survive, so that the forest is back in equilibrium. It's all about balance and equilibrium.

This system is backed up by miles and miles of mycelium – the fungus network. It's hard to verify all of this, unless you're an earthworm, a burrowing animal or an ostrich. But still, Suzanne Simard,[15] a professor from the University of British Columbia, did just that. She created an entire battery of tests aiming to demonstrate that trees are interconnected through

15 I highly recommend watching Suzanne Simard's TED Talk 'How trees talk to each other', given on 22 July 2016.

their roots. Over 30 years, her passionate research has proven the existence of 'mother trees' that feed carbon dioxide to younger trees through their roots, because the 'children' have limited access to light and carbon.

Dr Simard's research has also proved that root exchanges take place both between trees of the same species and between deciduous trees and evergreens – for example, between silver birch and Douglas fir. (Doug, I knew you were a great guy!) These two species don't absorb carbon at the same time of year, because they don't live according to the same rhythm (*see the Second Wisdom*), so one species helps the other through its 'shortage' season. And vice versa. Whether trees are weak or strong, they all need each other.

When some overly greedy logging companies cut down all of the silver birch around the Douglas fir, they forget how much happier fir are when they're with birch, because they exchange carbon, and so grow better and are more resistant to disease.

Hands Clasped

I have often felt alone in life and that no one really understands me. This has often been true. But whenever I've been drowning,

An invisible support network

I've always had a helping hand, such as my chance meeting with Sister Emmanuelle, the nun renowned for her work with the poor in Egypt and Turkey, on a train platform in Nice, or a writing class offered by a non-profit organization trying to give a confidence boost to people – like me – earning the minimum wage, or therapists, or doctors. Or the child who just came up to me in the street and laughed while imitating what I was doing, right down to the smallest gesture. If I scratched my head, he scratched his head. If I sat like the Buddha, so did he. Twin smiles: his and mine.

In my dark times, the hands of the human family have been there for me. And I've often reached out for them. I've been so grateful for them.

Sometimes humans haven't been there, but Doug has been, and the spruce, and other trees too.

Epilogue: Only One Human Consciousness

And how about you? Do you feel connected to other people? Not only to your close friends and family, but to strangers? Deep inside, do you feel connected to your family, your village, your city, your region, your country? To your planet? Are you aware of breathing the same air as everyone else? Of being nourished by the fruits and vegetables that the air and earth produce? Most of all, are you aware of your roots? Are you aware of the roots of all of humanity?

Can you remember situations in your life when you spontaneously held out your hand to a stranger, or helped someone who was in trouble, or did something totally altruistic for a fragile living being? Just listening is a heroic act. Surely, simply by listening, by giving your attention to another living being, you've disrupted a few moments of your daily routine to take care of another living being, either one you love or one you've never met before.

At the same time, do you remember all of the hands that have been extended to you: by your parents, teachers, children, by strangers, and also by animals – pets or wild creatures?

Think of all of those gestures. There are a lot of them, right?

Maybe you've even helped someone you couldn't stand who was in the middle of a crisis. Have you noticed how hard times bring us together?

Regardless of the circumstances, maybe you've met people who are very different from you and noticed the richness of the interactions that you've been able to have with them. Different ways of thinking, of being, of acting, can be inspiring, can't they? New perspectives? Gifts?

EXERCISE

CONNECT WITH OTHERS

Now is the time to connect with a living being that is unlike you, that is your opposite.

If you're a fir, go and find a spruce or another sun-loving tree: a pine, an oak, a larch. And if you're a spruce, go and look for a shade-loving tree: a fir, a beech or a hornbeam. (*For a list of sun- and shade-loving trees, see footnote page 34.*)

Greet your tree, then ask its permission to do the exercise with it.

If it agrees, immediately make physical contact with it: touch it with your hand, your arm, your cheek, your forehead or your entire body. As soon as you're feeling balanced, begin INEX breathing (*see page 34*), then feel your roots extending down through your feet (*see page 35*). Feel how this creates a connection between you and the living being that is unlike you. Savour the difference.

After a few moments, add a third step to your INEX breathing: as you inhale, puff out your belly or feel as if your inhalation is reaching down into your pelvis.

Feel this new sensation of deep breathing while maintaining your INEX breathing and your roots.

Let this moment last as long as feels right to you.

When you've finished, thank the tree that is so different from you. One day, it may be lending you a hand. If you can, if you want to, give it a name.

TIME TO CREATE

Immediately after this session with your third tree, go back to your INEX breathing for a few moments. Then let the words flow out of your belly and your internal organs.

~ A SPRUCE, CONFRONTED BY GRAVITY ~

Spruce,

Your branches hang, your cones hang.

Haven't they fed your fiery spirit?

The spirit of your trunk, that shoots forth like a geyser?

The spirit of your tallest branch, which pierces the clouds?

Who holds them down? What force weights them?

EXERCISE

INEX+ BREATHING

During the spring, you have come into contact with the major types of trees and their personalities: trees that attracted you without necessarily being like you; trees that were exactly like you; and trees that were your opposite. You've experienced the feelings that these contacts, whether distant or intimate, brought up in you.

At the same time, you've practised making a connection to yourself through nasal breathing, through anchoring yourself to the Earth and through belly breathing. I call that process INEX+ breathing.

At any point in the day, you can use INEX+ to connect with these three powerful anchor points and feel grounded and centred. When you're commuting, when you're at work, use INEX+. The memory of what you experienced with those three trees will help you.

And when you interact with another human being, ask yourself what type of encounter it is: attracting like-to-like or a meeting of opposites. When you shake someone's hand, activate the memory of touching the tree that was most like that person. Automatically go into INEX+ mode.

Little by little, as you practise this technique, you will appreciate how good it is to feel yourself breathing consciously and to feel anchored and centred in a variety of relationship situations. How good it is to feel supported by your trees.

Do it more and more. Let it become something you do automatically. Be present to the life within you.

SUMMER

A Time of Abundance

In summer, trees are majestic; they are leafed out in full abundance and they soak up every drop of sunlight that kisses them at the solstice. They savour the moment.

Spring has laid the groundwork and now everything is ready to reach its full potential. The first fruits of summer are ripening. The forest is bursting with life.

Trees revel in this. Trees always say *yes*. In many situations, they show us how they can adapt, how they can change course midstream and remain completely confident, how they can ride the trade winds. They are fully present during everything that happens in their lives. Now, in summer, they are maturing, before the harvest. It's a season flooded with light, and every living thing savours it. Projects that were begun in spring naturally come to fruition; we all feel laid-back, unstressed. Nothing can touch us.

What do you do in summer? The rhythms of our modern society mean that summer seems, on the surface at least, like a season of rest. But is it really? Unless you're lucky enough to have a job that is also your passion, your summer holiday is one of your rare chances to do what you really want to do – a time of real freedom, a time finally to live your dreams.

Whether you decide to climb a mountain or lie on a beach, you'll feel everything more intensely, simply because you're driven by your inner joy.

Summer is a time to reconnect to joy.

BE PRESENT

Have you ever been lost in your thoughts instead of experiencing what is really going on? Have you ever felt as if you're living in the past or the future, or in a dream world of your own making, rather than truly experiencing things that are hard, or just plain boring? **What a sweet intoxication to create a world where everything is exactly as you want, whether it's a living being or something inanimate.** How can you *not* dream of what you don't have, whether that's love, joy or money? Or of what has been taken away from you: someone you love, a physical ability, a house, a gift, a childhood? And then there are the hours spent trying to understand it all, in a whirlwind of thoughts, when you could be living. Simply living. It's odd, isn't it?

This film that rolls in our head, as wonderful as it may be, causes us to float above reality. It might be useful or even healthy when our reality is unbearable, but it's still a film. It's not reality, it's a mirage. Sooner or later, we have to face what we're avoiding if we want to move forward. If we want to feel free. If we want to avoid feeling stuck or having our dis-ease show in our body as symptoms or illness.

What do trees experience? The present, the past or an imaginary future?

What Tree Rings Tell Us

Have you ever seen the inside of a tree? Seen inside the bark, the branches and the leaves? Seen the heart of a tree? Seen who it really is?

Why not walk through a forest where some of the trees have just been cut down? With their insides showing, they can tell you their stories.

April 2017: I was preparing for the first RandOlyric musical walk of the spring, in the Gâvre forest in western France's Loire-Atlantique region, when I saw the stump of an oak tree. It had just been cut down. Age: 129 years. I'm sure of that, because I counted its rings twice, first from the centre to the outside and then back again. That tree could have lived a lot longer, but that's the maximum age that logging companies here allow oak trees to reach. Some people call it the 'rotation' age.

Its trunk had already been hauled away. I could see the still-fresh evidence: where it had fallen, where the chain saws had cut its branches off, where the tractor had skidded it so that it could be driven to a sawmill to be made into sawdust, furniture, a barrel or a piece of a wooden boat. I could still smell motor oil, and the tractor's massive tyres had churned the earth up like a World War I tank.

I thanked this oak for what it had given. I was seized with a desire to name it. Its name would be Gavry.

Gavry's Life

I decided to uncover more details about Gavry's life. I stared at his centre, the heart of his stump. Age: one year. Slowly, ring by ring, my laser-guided stare traced a radius to where Gavry had been cut down.

During the first years of his life, Gavry had grown quickly: his early rings were wide and generous. Then, after the age of 21, they decreased by almost half on the north side. The beech tree whose rotting stump I could see a few metres away must have caught him up in height and then outgrown him. Of course it was to the north.

Then Gavry had gone at it again. From 30 to 65, his rings hadn't grown as vigorously as during his first 20 years, but their growth had been wide and regular. In short, Gavry had had a peaceful life.

Then, at around the age of 80, I could see a black spot, which had caused his growth to slow temporarily. And there were annual growth rings only at that specific spot. A wound. A shock. Clearly, something hard and powerful had smashed Gavry. Maybe a branch or a trunk had fallen, or maybe Gavry had found himself alongside the path of an overly wide skidder. But in less than 10 years, he had rebounded from this injury and continued his life with honour until the age of 89.

Then, as he turned 90, all around the ring from that year I could see that his growth had slowed to a crawl. There was no doubt about it: this wasn't something specific to Gavry, nor was it a one-time external event. A world event must have affected him and all the trees of his generation. Later, I would see that confirmed by other stumps. Was it a particularly long and trying winter? An illness? Acid rain? A major drought? That seemed the most likely. Gavry's 90th birthday would have been more than 40 years in the past, so it would have been around the time of the great drought of 1976.

But Gavry had once again mustered the resources to survive that trial and continue living until the present day. He had even got a second wind in the last 20 years, probably thanks to the foresters who had cut down the beech and oak trees around him. Light had come back to him.

The Yearly Ring, Where the Sap Flows

As I squinted and peered at the stump, I remembered a story that people used to tell in the Dabo forest. A large deer had had the unfortunate idea of sheltering under a fir tree on a hot and stormy night, and a bolt of lightning had split the tree in two and killed him instantly. I never knew whether he was electrocuted or crushed by the trunk. And I never understood why no one had studied the death of the tree. I guess that shows the hierarchy of people's concern.

Maybe you've already come across a tree that has been split in two. Only lightning can do something like that. It's unfortunate, but it offers the rare chance to study the structure of a tree in greater depth.

First observation: most of the trunk is dead. The heart, the rings and a good part of the wood are completely dead. That's the part called the duramen. In some species, like oak or Douglas fir, the duramen is darker – brown or reddish – than the rest of the wood, which remains white or light-coloured.

So where is the living part?

The most intensely alive part of a tree is the cambium – the current year's ring – which will be growing before you. It's found in the outside part of the trunk, just inside the bark. That's where the sap circulates with all its might in the spring. There, on the heart side of the tree, it creates wood called sapwood. And further out, it creates bark called phloem.

When you see a tree that has just been cut down, you can immediately see that the past – the duramen and the sapwood – is dead or dying, while the present – the cambium and the phloem – is alive.

Cambium and *liber* – another word for phloem – mean 'change' and 'freedom' in Latin. What beautiful words to describe life!

🌿 THE LAYERS OF A TREE 🌿

Going from the tree's heart outwards, here are the various circular layers of the trunk:

~ The duramen: Heartwood; it is dead. In most trees (oak, Douglas fir), it is brown or red. In some trees (ash, maple, fir, spruce), it remains light in colour. The duramen makes up 75 per cent of the trunk.

~ The sapwood: Alive but dying (it takes 4–20 years to become duramen), this white wood makes up 20 per cent of the trunk.

~ The cambium: The current year's living ring, this forms the sapwood on the heart side and the phloem on the bark side; it makes up 2 per cent of the trunk.

~ The bark: Formed of phloem (living) and suber (dead), it makes up 3 per cent of the trunk.

These percentages vary from one species to another.

🌿

Interlocking Layers

If we take a 3D view, like the view of a tree that's been struck by lightning, we realize that **a tree's trunk is a hollow living cone that interlocks with a solid dead cone.** That's how a tree grows and grows each year, getting bigger in the same way as a Russian Matryoshka doll. A tree's extremities – its limbs and its highest branched – replicate this phenomenon: they are 'micro-trunks' that allow leaves, buds, flowers and fruit to thrive.

What Sustains Us?

What do trees offer us? The urgency of the present moment and a call to connect with the essence of life. So many wise sayings already express this.

Trees also teach us that there is a transition time, a time of mourning between the present and the past. The sapwood represents this. **Trees invite us to be patient and gentle, so that we can digest whatever happens to us.**

At the same time, we must take care not to cut ourselves off from the past.

In the course of my personal growth, I have often heard people say that we should live in the moment, only the moment and nothing but the moment. At times, I've even made the mistake of thinking that I could turn the page on my past by trying to cut myself off from it, detach myself from it … rip myself away from it.

I've been to the ends of the Earth, thinking that my past wouldn't come along in my suitcase. I've burned relics, buried symbolic objects, destroyed watches, thrown letters weighted with rocks into the ocean. It has all just been an illusion. I've felt relieved, but it has been fleeting. The past may seem to have gone, but it has still been there, in every cell in my body, in my thoughts and in my heart.

What I've forgotten is what trees physically show us: the past is dead, but the living rests on top of it. The present is the hollow, living cone on top of the solid, dead cone. The past is a pedestal, a solid base, even with its wounds and rifts, even with its lost happiness. It gives meaning and direction to our life. It is what supports us as we move towards the light. It is the richness of our experience, regardless of what we've been through.

Trying to move forward without being at peace with our past means living like a hollow tree, exposed to the wind and to parasites.

Clearly, Gavry's stump showed the extent to which he lived in the present and nothing but the present. It was all there, right before my eyes: the summer droughts, the moments of light and the seasons of shadow. Nothing was denied or sugar-coated. It all helped Gavry to grow.

Epilogue: Cones of Life

So, is a tree a cone of life surrounding what is dead (in other words, the present, surrounding the past), with the past supporting the present? What do you think?

And you, are you cutting yourself off from the present? If so, you're living in the movie version of your lost past or your imaginary future, and you're missing out on life now. In survival mode, this is helpful. You can put some distance between you and the hateful present, but it doesn't resolve anything. And furthermore, you're out of sync.

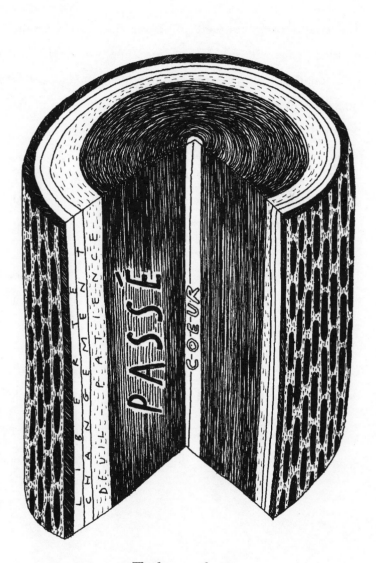

The layers of a tree
(from outside: freedom, change, patience and mourning, past and heart)

Are you cutting yourself off from the past without making peace with it? If so, you're cutting yourself off from your foundations, from what is supporting your life at this very moment and from the energy you need to reach your full potential.

Treating yourself very gently and very patiently, simply observe yourself. Differentiate between the moments when you're swimming in the water of the past, or the future, and the moments when you're embracing the present. For this, use INEX+ breathing (*see page 51*). Feel the nuances of this, and experience the effects. Consciously choose the quality that you want to bring to your life.

Like an arrow piercing the sky, your trunk shows you the direction to take, regardless of whether it is hollow, dense or full.

You are alive.

EXERCISE

BE PRESENT WITH YOURSELF

Go and search for your own Gavry in a forest that has just been thinned or logged. Choose a nice stump, preferably but not necessarily from a species that resembles you.

Greet the stump, ask it for permission to do the exercise with it, give it a name and thank it for its contributions.

Look at its life for a few moments – its calm periods, its tumultuous periods and its injuries – as I did with Gavry. Let its rings speak to you.

Then sit down on it, with your sit bones in balance on the wood. Feel good.

Begin doing INEX breathing: inhale and exhale as you grow roots down from your feet and also from where your sit bones are in contact with the wood. Feel your roots pushing down into the earth with every out-breath.

Then feel yourself moving into INEX+ breathing, filling your belly with your breath and feeling your spine undulating with your breath, like the trunk of a young tree.

The stump and its roots are supporting you, and you are its trunk.

After a few moments, get up. Can you feel the strength of your roots? Know that you are powerfully anchored to the Earth. With your feet shoulder-width apart, find a new equilibrium by moving your pelvis slightly. Stabilize yourself.

Feel the space between your legs as a solid cone on which your entire body, from your feet to your pelvis, is resting. Do a few moments of INEX+ breathing and feel the difference – in terms of density and solidity – that this makes.

Continue for as long as you like. Then thank this tree that has just died.

TIME TO CREATE

✎ Go back and sit on your stump again. Then go into INEX+ mode for a few moments and let the words flow out of you.

~ OPEN BOOK ~

You have died, but you still speak to us,

A book with all its pages open at once.

No paper, no pictures, no cover.

Just a few lines inspired by the ring.

Is there still life within you?

GO WITH THE FLOW

Cambium. **Life is change. Life is movement.** A series of events – expected or unexpected – that shape us over time. In the face of this truth, we have a choice: resist change, attempt to believe in the illusion of 'forever' and cling to certainties, or learn to float on the breeze that caresses the forest canopy.

And how do trees react to changes, to all the different elements?

The Beech Trees on the Ridge

When there's a storm on the main ridge of the Vosges mountains, everything happens at once: clouds cling to the hillsides; blizzards sand-blast everything in their path; snow takes pleasure in suffocating everything; hail shreds bits of leaf and bark before tearing into you as well. I don't know how the trees stand it. I've tried, and I haven't been able to last half an hour up there.

But the beech trees on the ridge, they survive. They bear the brunt of this extreme climate year round and they've found a way to survive better than any other deciduous or evergreen species at this altitude in the Vosges.

What's their secret? They fit perfectly into their environment. They've adapted to it. They've embraced their destiny. In addition to the exceptional resilience built into their DNA, they've learned to go with the flow of life around them. They've twisted and turned themselves and slimmed themselves down, so that the wind cannot take hold of them. You might say that they're dancing on the ridge, all leaning in the same direction, waving their shrunken arms adorned with dwarf leaves in rhythm with the seasons. They're natural bonsai trees. They might be 100 years old and only three metres tall. Unless you look carefully, you might not even realize that they're beech trees.

They're tough, those mountain beech. Because their growing season is so short, their wood is forged from such small rings that they're basically petrified in place, hard as stone. To survive up there, that's what they have to be like.

Humans have recognized their exceptional characteristics and given this area protected status. What an acknowledgement.

Snake Trees

Other trees use a different strategy to deal with two types of weather that can hit them at once: snow and sunshine. On the Vosges' steep slopes, it's not unusual for there to be more than a metre of snow at 1,000 metres. So, fir, spruce, maple, larch … whatever the species up there, they look like dancing cobras.

It's magical! From the base of the stump, the tree, whatever it is, traces a curved line, pauses for a few moments at the soil line, then progressively takes on a sensual waviness. And it's a practical sensuality. The shrubs on the plains or the flat summits that drown under three metres of snow with no lateral pressure on their trunks just can't understand it. But it's simply a matter of force. Double the weight, double the pain for the trees that live on the steep slopes of the Alsace plain's rift valley.

We can only imagine what the young trees go through here. Take a tender, supple sapling roughly three pine cones high. Imagine its very first winter, the curve that's forced on its trunk, or rather its stem, because it's still just a branch. It sleeps for four or five months under the snow, bent over … and that leaves a mark forever. It may be foolhardy and pop back up during the summer months, but the next winter will tame its pride and push it over again. It doesn't have a choice: it has to adapt.

These young trees can reassure themselves, though. They're not alone. None of their siblings or cousins escapes this fate. They're all crawling. They're all becoming 'snake trees'…

When they're taller than the deepest snowfall, they stand back up, with dignity, and they stand tall. It was just a detour … but one that will be imprinted on them forever.

Doug and His Brothers

Doug has always been a strong presence in my life. When I founded RandOlyric, which was based on the five senses, I had to find a particularly fragrant species of tree, one with a scent that would bring a feeling of wellbeing and linger for a long time in the memories of our nasal cells.

'Snake trees' moving along

As I walked down the first RandOlyric trail, Doug caught my attention. Or at least his scent did, floating like a ribbon through the air. Finding a Douglas fir, I cut off a tiny branch, thanking the tree that gave it to me, and I rubbed it between my hands. As I held it in front of my nose, Doug's soul was already entering my body. When I leaned over and opened up my hands, so full of his scent, like a cradle, I felt the same ecstasy that I had experienced when I had met Doug for the first time, 30 years before.

THE PERFUME OF THE FOREST

All plants produce and exude volatile odour molecules, trees included, although our untrained noses may not always notice their discreet and subtle scents.

There is one notable exception to this: the eucalyptus. If you walk into a stand of eucalyptus, you will immediately notice the scent of menthol wafting through the air.

Apart from this, the smell of conifers is always the easiest to pick up. Douglas fir have a gentle, fruity scent. And fir in general have the most lemony scent. Their spruce cousins exude an orangey resin.

Fir sap and Scots pine sap are known for their ability to relieve coughs and decongestion, often in the form of essential oils. Cedar wood provides a lovely scent for our drawers, and it also repels any mites that might dare to try and live in them.

Broadleaf trees are harder to identify by scent. Shade-loving trees such as beech and hornbeam tend to smell like humidity or moss. This is also true of the species that gravitate towards wetlands, such as poplar, aspen, alder and willow.

In 2002, in a French university study, six people assessed the scent of shavings from 288 oak trees. The researchers learned that the scent of coconut, vanilla, cloves, hay, new wood and even 'a pharmacy' could be detected, depending on the species and where it was growing. For example, wood from the trunk of an oak smells more like coconut or vanilla than wood from a branch, which tends to smell more like hay.

It's fascinating to read such research, but always go by your own experience. Put your nose on the trunk or the bark of beech, hornbeam, fir, Douglas fir, oak and maple and smell the difference. And experience these species in other ways too: smell their leaves, branches, fruit and cones. Smell the inner layers of a freshly cut tree.

The forestry school at Poisy-Annecy took us to all four corners of France to experience its diverse forests.

Once we went to Alsace, to the Hohwald forest, which had been a real haven for me as a child. But I hadn't been able to spend a lot of time there and I had walked right past the Douglas firs. Now, after spending the night in a youth hostel housed in an old pink sandstone castle, we were warned that we would soon be meeting some remarkable beings, the most impressive of their species.

It was an incredibly humid day. Our youthful exuberance spilled over as we walked along the path, which was covered with rust-coloured pine needles. **After some 15 minutes of walking, we detected a scent. It overpowered the already strong scent of the fir and spruce trees.** It reminded me of lemon balm, mixed with a whiff of orange and bergamot. The closer we got, the more we noticed overtones of liquorice and grapefruit, then all of these scents mixed together.

Suddenly we found ourselves in the nave of an enormous Gothic cathedral, with a 65-metre-high ceiling above us. And the giants welcomed us in all their majesty. They were straight and powerful. Their bark had blistered and cracked with the never-ending force of their growth. Planted in 1885, when this region had been annexed by Germany, they were living proof of the species' adaptability. Douglas fir grow at an unbelievable rate, with deep root systems like fir and broad trunks like spruce. Their needles decay to form soil that is richer and less acidic than that made by their native cousins. Doug ... you have so many incredible qualities.

Here's an important detail: although the Douglas fir is part of the *Pinaceae* family, it is neither a fir nor a spruce. It is a *Pseudotsuga*, a sort of hemlock.[16] Its Latin names are *Pseudotsuga douglasii* or *Pseudotsuga menziesii*; its common names are the Douglas fir, the Oregon pine and the Columbian pine.

Its needles are soft and bursting with scent, while its cones remain fairly small and have bracts shaped like a three-pointed lizard tongue. They are easy to recognize on the ground.

Foresters have studied the Douglas fir a great deal in recent decades, especially researchers from the French universities INRA[17] and IRSTEA,[18] which used to be called

---

16 Eastern hemlock are native to North America: their Latin name is *Tsuga canadensis*.

17 France's National Institute of Agronomic Research.

18 France's National Research Institute for Environmental and Agricultural Science and Technology.

CEMAGREF.[19] Because of its many positive qualities, it has been widely planted in the Vosges, in Brittany, in the Morvan, and throughout the Massif Central. I also – miraculously – found it on the banks of the river Rhine in Germany, just across the border from Alsace, when I was preparing my RandOlyric walk that focused on German Romanticism. The lava of the extinct Kaiserstuhl volcano seemed to have provided it with a favourable environment.

The Douglas fir is particularly resistant to disease and pests. It produces wood that is beautiful, solid and resistant to decay. A good number of my friends live in western France, in Bouvron, near Nantes, and they've used it to build their houses. Maybe someday soon, I will do that too. In any case, Doug is one of the species that grounds me. He is one of the foundations of my life as a forester and as a singing hiking guide for RandOlyric. I owe him so much.

Non-Natives Give Us So Much

Doug is a shining example of an introduced species. He isn't native to France, or even Europe. His seeds crossed an

---

19 France's Centre for the Study of Agricultural Mechanics and Rural Water and Forestry Engineering.

ocean to get here. His home is in the American and Canadian west where he's broken all kinds of records, growing more than 100 metres tall and to 12 metres in circumference.

He is truly a force of nature.

That's what we're connecting to when we take a Douglas fir twig in our hands and sniff it.

Many other species have also been successfully introduced to different places. This is true of the acacia, or more correctly the locust tree, or 'false acacia', whose French name, *robinier*, comes from the name of King Henry IV's botanist, Jean Robin. The locust tree was another American that crossed the seas during the age of the great explorers and rapidly colonized France. It was a pioneer!

In Alsace, I've seen locust trees in the middle of a grove of chestnut trees on the edge of a vineyard. They're nearly decay-proof, so they make excellent wood for vineyard stakes.

In Burundi, I was fascinated by the incredibly rapid growth of the eucalyptus trees that my predecessors from ISABU, Burundi's Graduate School of Agronomy, had planted at the

Manga forest station. I was responsible for measuring them. In 10 years, they could be more than 30 metres tall, meaning that they had grown at least three vertical metres per year. And all while they were so very far from their Australian homeland.

The Limits of Adaptation

Although trees often show incredible imagination and creativity as they adapt to a new climate or to being uprooted, this isn't always successful. *Some roots never take hold.* Some trees in a grove can't hold up under a lot of pressure. Some are fragile because the soil is too compact or they can't get enough moisture. Even Doug, one of the giants of this world, has his Achilles heel. If he's planted in soil that is high in limestone, he will quickly dry out and die. A few other species share this characteristic: the chestnut, the cork oak and some types of eucalyptus. We call them 'calcifugal'.

Additionally, climate change is making its mark on the modern era. There is a risk that many species will bump up against the limits of the climate and transitional phenomena will become more apparent. We shouldn't be surprised to see more disease, more yellow leaves or more bare branches in our forests.

But nature will adapt. Some species will disappear, but they will make room for others.

Epilogue: We Are Nature

What conditions do you thrive in? What pressures does your environment face and how do you react to them?

Like the mountain beech that bends before the howling wind, like the fir that becomes a snake under the weight of the snow, like the Douglas fir that knows how to adapt, you will adapt better when you ground yourself in nature and respect its rules. This will help you respond better in all circumstances. Also, by respecting nature, you respect yourself. And if you learn to detect every change in nature, you will learn to respond immediately to change. You will learn to adapt as best you can.

Once again, this brings us back to being fully present. And whether our relationship with nature is intimate or not, it is one of the keys to refining our reaction to any situation.

The exercise below invites you to use your full range of breathing as you prepare yourself to cope with anything that life throws at you. From the simplest part of the exercise (inhaling) to the most delicate (emptying your lungs and holding your exhale), as you breathe, you will see that you can adapt to every situation and that the more you experience a situation, the more comfortable you become with it. The exercise requires you to be fully present.

EXERCISE

LEARN TO BREATHE AT A DIFFERENT PACE

Walk into the woods and look for a tree. Base your choice on the mood you're in. Do you need to be reassured or are you ready to explore some differences?

As soon as you've chosen a tree, ask it for its permission to do this exercise.

Stand or sit with your back against the trunk and begin your INEX+ breathing (*see page 51*). Then explore something new: a four-step breath.

~ Inhale as you count to three.

~ With your lungs full of air, hold your breath as you count to three.

~ Exhale as you count to three.

~ With your lungs empty, hold your exhale as you count to three.

Do this at a speed that suits you. Truly feel each phase and feel your heart beating.

After a few moments, when you feel your initial rhythm becoming natural, increase your count to four.

Gradually, you can extend each phase to a count of five, or even 10. Welcome this progress, but always be sure to feel at ease with each count before you move on to the next. You're not trying to break any records; you're creating a habit. You're learning to feel good in all situations, and in all these four phases of life: inhaling (growing), holding your breath with your lungs full (maturing), emptying your lungs (shrinking) and pausing with your lungs empty (resting). Once you are used to the four-step breath, you won't fear any of these phases, whether they're symbolic or physical. Even when your lungs are empty and you are holding your exhale, you'll know what you are experiencing and be comfortable with it.

When you have finished, thank the tree.

Repeat the exercise soon.

TIME TO CREATE

When you have finished your four-step breathing, let the words flow out of you.

~ FOUR STEPS ~

Bend, do not break.

Make your mark, do not leave a scar.

Try, do not force.

Fly, do not hover.

Four steps, with no test.

MOVE FORWARD WITH CONFIDENCE

When do you allow yourself to be confident? If you're like most of us, it's when someone accepts you as you are and you see that they are reaching out to you. What about people who judge you, who put you down or who never reach out to you and are never there for you? You don't trust them, do you?

Now look inside yourself. What is your attitude towards yourself? Do you judge yourself? Do you put yourself down? Are you keeping the promises you've made to yourself? The promises you made when you were a child, or a teenager, and everything seemed possible? The resolutions you've made more recently to improve your physical and emotional health?

Keeping the agreements you've made with all the different parts of yourself is the key to self-respect.

Trees teach us that self-respect leads to self-confidence. In time, it becomes automatic. I learned that in a special forest.

The Risoux Forest

I've often lacked self-confidence. Because I've often given control of my inner life to my thoughts, my judgements and my emotions – to all the unstable elements of myself that I've identified with because I haven't been connected to the stable and aware parts of myself. Because I haven't been connected to the great empty space within.

For a long time I was so wrapped up in the lack of self-esteem that all of this caused, I really mistreated and rejected myself. **I completely forgot the promises that I'd made to the little boy that I had been.** I gobbled down junk food, I drank myself into oblivion and I persisted with the fantasy that other people were the cause of my unhappiness. I really believed that.

And then, one day, chaos. I had no choice: I had to wake up and go out into nature, into the forest with the First Nations of Quebec. I had to relearn how to live with myself. I had to regain my confidence.

Ten years later, when I was preparing a RandOlyric walk, I came across an extraordinary forest – the Swiss side of the Risoux forest. On paper, it's nothing much. It's mostly a stand of spruce, which can grow in the thin limestone-rich soil of the area. But somehow it's all come together to create an absolutely unique and exceptional forest.

There, in Switzerland's Joux valley, forestry workers care for the trees as they would a fine Swiss watch. They are like jewellers and the trees are great art, fine-tuned to the millimetre. How does that happen? Simply by sustainable forest management.

A Garden or a Tree Farm?

Very few foresters dare try sustainable forest management. It's time-consuming and expensive, and it demands an eye and a knowledge base that few people have.

Sustainable forest management is the art of cultivating a forest with trees of all ages. It promotes health, diversity, natural pruning and fine wood. Less wood is cut at any one time, but it's cut consistently and conservatively. There's no damage, no light or lack of light to traumatize the trees, no bands of sawn-off trees or clear-cuts. The forest looks more or less the same over time: thick, rich, sustainable. Incredibly strong.

Sustainably managed forests look like natural wild forests. Like the Wormspel forest. But they produce high-quality wood with no man-made gaps inside it.

A Forest of Resonant Wood

The Swiss foresters' lives are made infinitely more complex because they practise sustainable forest management. But it's worth it: the greatest instrument-makers in the world come to select their wood from the Swiss side of the Risoux forest. The native spruce that grow there have exceptional strength and acoustic properties. This is partially due to their genetic make-up, but also to the long and freezing winters of the Jura region, which cause the trees to grow in consistent, fine increments. You can see this very clearly when you peer down at a freshly cut spruce stump to count the rings.

The wood from this forest sings in the hands of violinists, violists, cellists, double bass players and guitarists. But not all of the trees from this 'singing forest' will have the honour of being selected for instruments. Only the straightest, the tallest, the most beautiful and those with the finest, most consistent rings will have that as their destiny. As usual, the other trees will be there to serve the special ones. Without a stable pony, there is no racehorse! In the Risoux forest, a few beech and fir (shade-loving trees) add value to the spruce (sun-loving trees), merely by being present.

Every Age Together

Because we find both shade- and sun-loving trees and every generation living together in this forest, we feel good there. Every nook and cranny allows us to observe every variant of life. Young trees grow vigorously under the watchful eye of the older and wiser trees, while 'middle-aged' trees take up space and link the other trees together in solidarity. No one is left behind.

In this forest, I feel connected to all of the phases of my life. I feel like saying 'I love you' to the baby I was. I feel like saying 'I love you' to the boy, the teenager and the young man I was. I don't leave out any of them, not even the man I was during the dark times. I see you, too; I feel what it's like to be

Trees of all ages

you, wounded and crying. I love you more than anything. I am a shooting star on fire with unconditional love. It comes from deep within me and it begins with how I feel about you. And about myself now.

As I think of you, I come across a young fir. It is twisted and contorted, with gashes in its bark from which sap is running out. It is so overpowered by the great spruces around it that it is shrivelled and stunted. I take it in my arms and hug it with all my might, feeling its soft branches caressing my face. I see my tears dropping onto the sap running down its bark. My tears melt into the sap, bandaging each of the wounds one by one. I hear the sound of my voice fill the space and echo off the bark of the other trees, reflected back from every pore of these illustrious 'singers'. I hear hundreds of violins, their music swelling in ascending spirals through the air around me and the tree.

Young fir, you know, and I know, that at this moment you are loved beyond measure.

Are Words Sacred?

In return, the tree gives me a scent – a scent that surrounds me, thrills me, just like the scent of the trees that welcomed me as I arrived at the First Nations cultural site Tsonontwan. There were spruce and fir there too.

Some of the first words that the Huron-Wendat chief said to me were, 'Word. Sacred.' As he explained, **it is important to be extremely careful with the words that leave our mouth, because they are connected directly to our being.** And we don't fool around with our being. This is also how we can grow our confidence. Having confidence in the integrity of our words means that we don't use words in the wrong way – we don't use them for false purposes, or for futile gains, or to make fun of people or judge them. We should be clear and precise with our words, and we should keep our word.

I leave the young fir, feeling nourished, whole and peaceful. On the way back, with each step I feel my breath like a balm of gratitude soothing all of the parts of me that I had acknowledged. They all understood that I was there to meet their needs, my needs, whether they were in the past or in the present moment. I gave my word of honour, and it was heard. I felt a real burst of self-confidence.

However, my aim of creating a RandOlyric walk in Switzerland did not come to fruition. None of the people I was hoping to meet were available when I was there. So be it. The gift was something else. The gift was meeting the trees. They were available to meet me.

Epilogue: Self-love

You are both the tree and the entire forest. Others might say that you are the wave and the ocean, the breeze and the air.

The point is, **the forest is All. It is awareness.** With this awareness, you can start to pick out each of your parts, each of your trees. The more attention you pay to each of them, especially those that make themselves known in a forceful way, the more you will feel the balm of peace and confidence inside yourself.

This became clear to me in the Risoux forest. Because it is so diverse, it clearly symbolizes the richness of our inner lives.

Welcome, acknowledgement, dialogue, words, love. The most beautiful gift we can give ourselves is being fully present to everything going on within us. Just as a mother or father is present for each of their children.

EXERCISE

FIND WHAT GROUNDS YOU

Take a walk in some mixed woodland. It doesn't really matter what types of tree you find there, or what forestry method is used. Just make sure that you can find a wide variety of species and ages.

As you walk, touch each tree along your path. If you feel like it, take a few detours to touch more trees.

Every touch is a reminder of your INEX+ breathing. If you've strayed from it, the reminder will bring you back. If you have kept up with it, the reminder will reinforce it.

After a little while, do the same thing while just 'touching' the trees with your eyes. This allows you to make contact with a huge number of trees and to walk easily while maintaining your INEX+ breathing. Then the breathing will become a habit.

When you breathe in this way, you are in contact with yourself. And the trees will reflect this back to you. You will make contact with the entire forest.

Later, when you are back in an urban environment, try to do this exercise again. It's amazing. Every time you see a tree, let it be a reminder. Breathe, ground yourself and you will know what to do.

You will see that even in cities, there are trees around to support us. What grace!

For now, when you leave the wood, turn back for a moment. Inhale deeply, thank the trees and say goodbye.

TIME TO CREATE

🖎 After this experience, feel the presence of your breath. Feel its full power. And then write.

~ YOUR FOREST ~

It is your mirror.

All of these beings are you.

Your parts, your entities, your creations.

Caress them with your eyes.

Embrace them with your fingers.

Draw them together with your heart.

Trust.

AUTUMN

A Time of Healing

After a summer of abundant experiences, autumn arrives. Little by little, easily and peacefully, the flow of energy decreases. Passions seem to burn less brightly and everything that seemed to happen without any effort becomes more work. It is time for the last harvests, the last rays of sun – red, yellow and orange. It is also the season when, if we do too much without recouping the energy we have expended, we can injure ourselves or become exhausted.

We go through the fire at this time. In Europe, the trees are on fire. Even more so in Quebec, where everything is more intense. And if you've ever seen the autumn colours of the maple or oak forests of North America, you'll know what emotions an entire hillside 'on fire' with turning leaves can inspire. Your heart pounds like a drum; your joy spirals up to the heavens; your breath is as warm as a yearling wolf.

It seems as if nature is trying to light an enormous, joyful bonfire to announce its great transformation. But there is no need for real flames in the forest. The wind blowing through the canopy is enough to create waves of red, yellow and orange, and to ruffle the branches that have been bearing the weight of these leaves since the first breaths of spring.

They have grown weary, and that's understandable.

Now the energy flow turns down instead of up. Soon, there will be too little light for photosynthesis and not enough pressure for sap to flow to the treetops. The upper branches will be in the clouds, too high up.

Soon the great sleep will begin.

But now the fire extends as far as the eye can see. The entire forest must burn, clean, incinerate everything that has grown and been tested.

Maybe something else is burning too – sorrow, anger and fears that have been hovering outside the veins of sap. It's not easy to leave behind the perfume of summer. It's not easy to sense that the flow of sap is drying up. It's not easy to let go.

And so the leaves light up the sky one last time. A final burst of energy brings the embers to life once more.

Then they die.

It's time to let go.

LEARN FROM YOUR MISTAKES

Trees in the forest see living beings moving all around them. For example in Quebec, there are deer, caribou, wolves, coyotes and people all using the same space. **Prey, predators and major predators all co-exist.** For all of them to live in harmony in one space, a fragile and subtle equilibrium must reign. The smallest disruption at the top of the pyramid can have significant – and sometimes irreversible – consequences.

So, in an indirect way, **trees show us the limits that we must respect** and invite us to learn from our mistakes.

A Sustainable Forest

In France, we're spoiled. Of course there are cuts that look too harsh, and clearings that look too dramatic, and smaller and smaller rotations. But **in general, French forests are fairly well managed, and always with an eye on sustainability.** As evidence of this, France's forested land totalled 14.6 million hectares in 1989, when I was at forestry school. Today it's somewhere around 17 million hectares, according to the National Institute of Geography. That's an increase of 0.70 per cent per year. That's cause for celebration, even though that increase says nothing about the change in the average age of the trees. They're undoubtedly younger now, because we don't let them grow for so long.

We can still hope that financial pressures won't affect the National Office of Forests' management policies, or the plans issued by the Regional Forest Centres.[20]

In other parts of the world, for example in the Amazon, Canada and Burundi, the situation is completely different. The crushing demands of the paper industry, combined with intensive

---

20 These regional branches of the French government's National Centre for Private Forests prepare management plans for private forests; these plans include healthy management of these areas, environmental protection, land management, etc.

agriculture and looting during disastrous political situations can ravage large swathes of forest. People make mistakes; that's how we learn. But does nature also make mistakes?

My First Trip to Quebec

The application process was rigorous. The competition was stiff, the discussions were heated and the wait was agonizing, because so many of us in my forestry class had applied. Our school had a partnership with the forestry school in Rimouski, on Quebec's Gaspé peninsula. The previous year, an exchange programme had begun. Now they had to find a successor for the first intern, who had come back amazed. Only one person would be chosen, and eventually … I was selected. I was so excited!

I was 21 years old. **It was my first big trip, my first flight and my first overseas work experience.** When I read the information about the six-month internship, one thing jumped out at me: the Quebecois weren't just using me for their own purposes. First, they were going to pay me well and give me free housing. Next, and most importantly, they had agreed to bend their policies a little by agreeing to one of my slightly odd requests: wolves.

Finally, I would have free rein to study survival strategies in forests with large numbers of cervids in winter. That would be the major part of my programme and would take place in the southeastern region of 'the beautiful province',[21] in the Eastern Townships. I was overjoyed.

Canis Lupus

I had been fascinated by wolves since I was a child. But what do wolves have to do with forests? To me, it was obvious then and is now: wolves eat deer, and deer eat young trees. **Managing the wolf population, and more generally the large predator population, has a significant impact on forest regeneration.**

I had convinced both my French and Quebecois professors that a study on that kind of predator in a forest made sense. However, a study on wolf populations in Quebec had already begun the previous year, so I decided to study their cousin the coyote and their comrade the black bear. This wasn't a bad Plan B. The study would take me into the heart of the Gaspé national park, where baby caribou went to vanish. This was truly a disaster,

---

21 As Canadians call the province of Quebec.

since the variety of caribou specific to the Chic-Choc mountains was threatened with extinction. There were barely 250 of them left. We urgently needed to identify their primary predator and then organize a hunting plan to restore the balance.

🌿 AN ATYPICAL CERVID 🌿

Caribou are the only cervids whose females also grow antlers. They are smaller than male caribou's antler racks, and they drop about six months after the males', when the baby caribou are born in the spring.

The Gaspé caribou are perfectly adapted to the alpine conditions in the Chic-Choc mountains. In the summer they eat grasses and lichen, and in the winter only lichen – both on the ground and on the trees. They are isolated from Quebec's other caribou populations and in 2017 they were designated as being threatened with extinction.

Coincidentally, the word 'caribou' comes from the Micmac[22] word *kaleboo*, or 'the one who paws'. Europeans refer to caribou as reindeer.

---

22 A First Nations people indigenous to northeastern North America.

Bear, or Coyote

The only way to identify the caribou's predators was to gather a large amount of coyote and black-bear scat and send it to a lab that would dry it out to look for baby caribou fur. The Quebec Ministry of Recreation, Fish, and Game did the job. Each morning, along with a few colleagues, I took off in a helicopter that deposited me on top of a mountain. Then I walked in a descending spiral pattern, using a specific statistical protocol. One day we went to Mont Albert, another day to Mount Logan and another day to Mount Jacques Cartier or another of the round peaks in the Chic-Chocs. They looked like my memories of the Vosges mountains, only without the man-made buildings and with an ocean. I soaked up the view.

There was so much scat! Every day, I gathered a sack full of it and marked on a map the exact site where I had found it. It was a mapped galaxy of animal droppings. Luckily, each species' was easy to recognize. Bears produced an amazing heap, while coyote scat looked like a cigar – not unlike that of their domestic cousin the dog.

As we flew back to the town of Saint-Anne-des-Monts in the evening, the pilots would sometimes see a huge pile of bear scat on the ground and land to collect it. The helicopter cost more than $3,000 an hour, so I can't even tell you the price per cubic centimetre of that scat!

In the end, we found that there was caribou fur in all of the scat that we gathered. The two predators ate similar numbers of young caribou.

Population control for the excess predators would stop the bloodshed.

Mankind's Fault

Unfortunately, the latest update shows that despite a slight improvement in the early 2000s, **the caribou's situation is still critical**. In September 2016, a journalist from the publication *Le Devoir* even wrote an article entitled 'Requiem for the Gaspé Caribou'. Today there are fewer than 100 left, compared to 250 at the beginning of the study.

It's easy to blame the bears and coyotes, but we always come back to the most destructive creature of all: humans. Over-tourism in the Chic-Chocs, and over-exploitation of the forests around the Gaspé park seem to have killed off the caribou slowly but irreversibly. What's more, the Earth has suffered from massive deforestation, which has been made easier and faster as machines have become more efficient.

A Mechanical Monster

Before I went to the Sherbrooke region to study the white-tail deer, I had to meet **one of the crown jewels of Canadian forestry: the machine that cut down trees and stripped them of their branches**. This was a hybrid monster, a kind of cross between a combine harvester and a giant Caterpillar bulldozer.

The logging company employees were proud to show me how quickly an entire forest could be clear-cut using this beast. The machine's enormous front 'jaw' cut the tree off at its base, then skinned it, like an enormous vegetable peeler. Finally, it cut it into logs that could be loaded on the paper mill's trucks. All of this took just a few seconds, without the machine ever letting go of the tree, the prey. So much for the chain saw. Exit stage left for the pruning saw. **This all-in-one machine reduced the forest to a harvested wheat field, devoured by the thundering monster.**

At the same time, perhaps to relieve its conscience, the government of Quebec had come up with a project: 'Trees for Tomorrow.' Like other students, I helped out with this for a couple of days. There were 3 billion evergreen trees to plant in the clear-cuts made by the hellish machines. It took 10 seconds to dig a shallow hole and put in a tiny tree whose taproot had been made into a cylinder shape. A little stomp of the foot to press the soil down around the plant, a quick prayer that the seedling stuck and there you were.

The intentions were good, but the project had limited effect. It was already too late. The soil was poor, robbed of its organic material, eroded by the gentlest shower, or flooded due to lack of roots to absorb the moisture.

It was a true desert. It would take decades for the forest to recover.

Many other mistakes are made to this day during reforestation projects. Trees are planted too close together, or in a monoculture, or the species that are selected are wrong for the climate or the soil. These attempts bring their own disequilibrium in the form of disease, or unstable trees that blow down in the slightest breath of wind, and biodiversity suffers.

Selective felling

Epilogue: Choosing How to Let Go

Have you ever chosen to 'clear-cut' your life? Have you ever completely cut yourself off from people or places? Have you ever tried to cut down, cut off or dissociate yourself from what you've been through? Have you ever given all of your energy to something, to the point where you were completely exhausted?

I've done that a few times. And it's worked! Sometimes it has resolved problems or brought me some short-term relief, but it has been brutal. It has had significant after-effects and I have taken longer to recover – if I have even had the resilience to do that. I've been exactly like a forest that's been replanted in one fell swoop. A forest like that is in shock: the soil is poor; there are floods; things are fragile and eroded, and it takes a long time for them to grow back. See how each of those words equates to something that we feel as humans: shock, fatigue, tears, fragility, emptiness and slow recovery.

It's too much. It might produce noticeable results, but it's too much, too fast, and we pay for it later.

Now I feel like trying new methods – slower, softer transitions, clearing things out bit by bit, harvesting with respect, with love for biodiversity, like the Risoux forest. It's a conscious choice that I've made through trial and error, and it offers the option of more responsible decisions. It's a simple philosophy: experiment, and then make changes if needed.

Nature doesn't make mistakes. Everything contributes to its balance. No wolf, bear or coyote is responsible for what we do.

EXERCISE

LOVE YOURSELF AS YOU ARE

~ Deep in the forest, go to see your friend, the tree that is most like you. It is important that you feel fully confident. It is also important that you are alone – free, with no one around you.

~ As you greet your tree friend, ask if it is open to having you there. If so, lean back against it, with the back of your head pressed against its bark.

~ Anchor yourself to the ground and begin your INEX+ breathing (*see page 51*). Moment by moment, feel the wave of your spinal column pressing against the tree trunk and relaxing again.

~ When you've established your INEX+ breathing, turn and take the tree in your arms. Close your eyes.

~ This tree is you. Embrace yourself with all your might. Embrace all your imperfections and your mistakes. Your only mistakes have been not knowing, and you are doing everything you can not to repeat those mistakes.

~ Use INEX+ to greet any thoughts or judgements that come up. Welcome any tears or emotions. Let them live.

~ Continue embracing the tree. Physically try to touch its bark and its wood with your heart.

~ Give every out-breath up to the air or the earth.

~ Continue for as long as you want.

~ Breathe.

~ Then thank the tree.

TIME TO CREATE

Afterwards, write about a difficult experience you have had. You could do this in the form of a letter to yourself, or to anyone you want.

~ A Little Too Much ~

Too much. I loved you too much.

I understood too late that it wasn't love,

Just a calling,

Just a chasm to cross…

And you couldn't do anything about it.

Tree, help me to love,

Truly love.

Turn Injury into Opportunity

Trees are like us; they get hurt, sometimes seriously. In the face of adversity, they've developed a full range of solutions, and they've created strategies to defy death's fickle, fatal caress. From the tiniest scratch to a defiant cry of survival, they are determined to bounce back. They love life so much that life supports them to the very end – delaying, breathless, the inevitable final moment.

What is your mindset when you get injured, whether in body or soul? Have you noticed that healing depends on how you look at things?

Of course, you can heal yourself with mainstream medicine. But do you drag your feet like a victim or do you observe how a scar forms with the wonder of a newborn child? Do you swear with all your might or do you cultivate that great treasure, patience?

Trees remain calm during their time of healing.

First Steps at Island Brook

During my internship in Quebec, I found myself in Sherbrooke, the tranquil capital of the Eastern Townships, just over the border from the United States. I had barely arrived at the Ministry of Recreation, Fish, and Game when I was given an office and a company car – a right royal welcome. That region's French origins are certainly good for something!

But even though – on the surface – Quebec's social codes are borrowed from France's, and the language is similar, and the few old houses look like those in Brittany, I was definitely in North America.

I was thrilled to have an energetic office mate who gave me advice on a daily basis. Especially when I learned that my research would take place on private land in the municipality of Island Brook and I would have to talk to various landowners in English, due to its proximity with the USA. Would my basic secondary-school English do the job? In my heart, I had some reservations.

Deer Yards

Island Brook is a special forest. It has areas called 'deer yards', which are the winter habitat of the white-tailed deer. In those spots, the climate is less harsh and the deer can find food and shelter.

White-tailed deer[23] are nothing like European deer. They're smaller, with brown fur, the colour of a squirrel's, and lighter-coloured antlers that curve forwards. Their antlers tend to be smaller than those of the larger male red deer in Europe or western Canada.

What goes on inside a deer yard? The Quebec winter is so long and harsh, and the snow so deep, that the deer have to invest in more elaborate survival strategies than their cousins in more temperate climates. There's no heating, and no fresh food for six months. The temperature can go down to minus

---

23 White-tailed deer are so called because of their tails, which stand up like white flags when they are running.

35° Celsius. To survive and even move around in more than one metre of snow, the deer use their hooves to paw out trenches. They huddle together to stay warm, and they take advantage of the walls of snow that form a sort of thermal insulation like the walls of an igloo. They live in a kind of open-air hotel!

The trickiest issue for them is finding food. There's not much to eat in winter, so they eat young trees: bark, dormant or new buds and the tender, tenacious needles of evergreen trees. They completely strip the trees – scalp them! It's easy to recognize trees that have been 'buzz cut' by deer – they're like a band of punk rockers!

Forked and Twisted

I'd seen these kinds of injuries on European trees, but never so many in one place. One of the most common was caused by the removal or death of the tree's uppermost bud. Whether it was gobbled down by a deer or succumbed to a late frost, it was a 'head wound' for the tree.

How could a young tree reach for the sky without its highest bud? It risked not reaching its full potential.

But I soon saw that a tree like this was able to compensate; it was able to adapt. **The call of the light was so strong that other buds would take over.** If there wasn't an available bud on the crown, then others, lower down, would rise up, working like crazy, energetically welcoming the flow of sap that would automatically head towards them after the uppermost one had died.

Sap, rising like a geyser, needs somewhere to go. It has to find life-giving openings. When it does, it will explode through them.

Of course, this can make a tree look a little off-kilter and rickety, or even twisted. If a tree is perfectly symmetrical, on the other hand, there's a good chance that it's a maple or an ash, because their buds grow symmetrically. Beech trees have alternating buds, and their forks are crooked and not symmetrical at all. Other trees, like oaks and chestnuts, grow somewhat randomly.

Quebec: The Grand Finale

Quebec spoiled me – many of the landowners in Island Brook, not to mention the deer in the deer yards, came out to meet me.

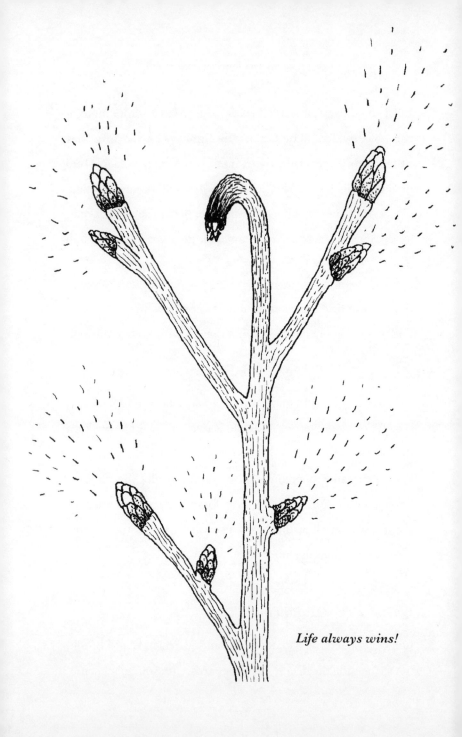

Life always wins!

My schoolboy English proved to be good enough. Everyone tried their best to communicate with me, speaking slowly and carefully.

My internship ended with a bang. My colleagues in Sherbrooke encouraged me to spend my final week on Anticosti Island, a haven for white-tailed deer at the point where the Saint Lawrence river meets the sea and you can't tell which is which.

After many hours on the bus, I reached the small city of Sept-Îles and then made a dash for the first ferry to Port-Meunier, the tiny 'capital city' of Anticosti. Its name comes from the famous *chocolatier* Meunier, the former owner of the island, who introduced a small herd of deer to it. Since then, the animals have multiplied, and many hunters go to the island today to save the trees from being eaten alive.

My first few hours on Anticosti certainly confirmed the problem. Teetering along on a mountain bike, I came across deer every five minutes or so – entire herds of them, including does with their fawns and huge bucks with antlers like petrified tree branches. All around me, spruce trees, chewed to bits by the hungry deer, seemed to have sacrificed themselves to ensure the white-tailed deer's survival.

At night, I slept in a camper owned by a man who lived out in the woods. As a summer job, he counted the salmon swimming up the river. Every day the same routine, every day the same silence, the river mist, the dampness, the eddies. He was happy.

One night when I couldn't sleep, I went down to the river bank, drawn by the light of the full moon. **There, silhouetted in the moonlight, a silver fox was fishing for salmon, swiping confidently with his paw.** Either he was too small or the salmon too big, though. I never saw him land one, but he moved with grace and intent. For that fox, nothing else existed. Not even me, a two-legged intruder from a nowhere town in France.

My heart melted.

Supermodels

Back in France, I took a job in a commercial forest in Wangenbourg, in the Vosges. The big Scots pines there were very high quality. Their bark dotted with orange at the top of the trunks, **they stood perfectly straight, with few branches and few suckers.** If they had been human, they would have been supermodels.

On skidding day, things happened quickly. The tractor pulled the 30-metre trunks along like matchsticks. Sometimes the trunks would brush against the trees alongside the road, but those trees seemed to have been made to stand it. They were like pillars guarding the way for the huge pines being dragged along the ground. And they certainly weren't unscathed.

In the forest, you often come across trees that have been skinned alive: a piece of their bark – small or large – has been ripped off. Maybe a branch has fallen on them, or maybe they have been scratched by a tree trunk during a hasty skidding operation. Maybe a teenager has carved a heart and their initials into the bark. And then there are insects, worms, larvae and woodpeckers all chomping and pecking away... So many reasons for an injury, and only one cure: fill in the gap and carry on. Just as with human skin. Because an open wound is dangerous. It can be infiltrated by parasites or pathogens; it can rot if water and air get in. That's how a tree becomes hollow: the sapwood and the duramen break down. So you have to act quickly ... or as quickly as a tree can.

Sap does the trick. **In the vicinity of the wound, the cambium steps up its production of sap** and creates a surplus of phloem, which turns into bark and fills the hole. This creates a thick scar, and will be enough for a wound that isn't too large.

The large pines in Wangenbourg, along with most conifers, have a second substance that helps them heal. It's not sap, and it has no nourishing role – it flows through its own channels in the wood. **It is resin. It forms very tough scar tissue**, protecting the tree until bark covers the wound.

Epilogue: Helping the Healing Process Along

How many times have we clung to what we have lost, like the trunk bud that we thought was the only one that could help us grow … until it was gobbled up by a deer? So often we have a morbid attachment to what is no more. And if we haven't mourned those things, we can't see the new buds that are waiting for the green light.

In these situations, we have a choice: helping life along by accepting the pace of the healing process, or resisting and remaining tied to what we had before we were wounded.

Do you see yourself in one of these scenarios? What do you tend to do when they arise? Do you usually go with the flow of life, with the natural forces, the opportunities, that will arise all on their own if you let them?

EXERCISE

HEAL YOURSELF

When you're out walking in the woods, notice the wounds on the trees. Notice their broken forks, bark, branches...

Find a mid-sized evergreen tree, preferably one without sharp branches, like a fir or a Douglas fir. If you can't find one, a spruce will do the trick – but it will poke you!

Greet the tree. Ask it for its permission to do the exercise with it.

If it gives you permission, take a tiny fragment from one of its branches and hold it in the palm of your hand.

Stand and face the tree and begin INEX+ breathing (*see page 51*). Anchor yourself firmly to the ground and let things flow.

When you feel grounded, rub the twig between your hands for a few seconds. Then quickly bring your cupped hands up to your nose. Press your nose to your hands and breathe deeply.

Take a few breaths. Experience the essential oil. Let it heal you.

Do this every time that life wounds your heart a little.

Experience this for as long as you want.

Breathe.

Thank the tree.

TIME TO CREATE

🖎 You have noticed wounds – trees' wounds and your own. You have breathed in the healing power of trees. Now let the words flow out of you.

~ FRAGRANCE ~

The scent of resin,
These fleeting scents,
You heal my heart.

TURN AN ENDING
INTO A REBIRTH

There are wounds that are like stakes through the heart. There are points of no return. There are tunnels so long that not only light is lost, but the memory of light. **There are abrupt break-ups and separations, when we are torn apart.** There are moments when we feel dead and buried.

Trees experience all this too. Some don't survive, others struggle to survive and others defy all the odds and go on to live a life that goes far beyond what happened before.

They are our inspiration.

Trees in the Vineyards

In October 2010, I was making my way up a steep slope in a vineyard in France's Munster valley. It was the highest vineyard on Hohneck mountain, the third highest of the Vosges mountains. **I had hesitated before holding a RandOlyric walk in a vineyard, but then I had allowed myself to be convinced.** I had to admit, the surroundings were less wild than usual and the granite less impressive. But singing in a wine cellar filled with Riesling or Gewürtztraminer vapour was more than enough to make up for that. Whenever I go back, I always choose a path that goes through some forest sections, though. There can't be a RandOlyric walk without trees – that's non-negotiable.

In the area around the vineyard, everything contributes to the finished product: fine Alsatian wine. Trees do their part. For example, chestnut trees grow quickly and produce rot-resistant wood that makes excellent vine stakes.

Once, when I was above the vineyards in Wihr-au-Val, I found myself in a chestnut grove. The trees all looked alike, and they had all been cultivated in the same way by the vintners. Every stump had grown three, four, five or sometimes even six or seven branches that had, over time, become trunks. Foresters call this kind of grove a coppice.

🌿 THE ART OF CUTTING 🌿

Aside from sustainably managed forestry, as in the Risoux forest in Switzerland, there are three main ways of managing a forest: as a coppice, as a regular woodland and as a coppice with standards.

In a coppice, the trees grow like shrubs, with many shoots coming out of one stump. This is the result of buds coming to life when a tree is cut down. Simple coppicing is when all of the trees are cut down at once. Selective coppicing is when different trees are cut down at different times. Either way, coppicing produces low-quality wood for fence posts or firewood.

A regular woodland is a forest in which single-trunked trees, usually of the same species, grow from seeds or seedlings that have been naturally sown or planted. It produces lumber of varying quality for a variety of purposes – construction, boats, woodworking, veneer, parquet, panelling or posts.

A coppice with standards has both single-trunked trees and shrub-like trees. It is managed to produce lumber and firewood, and the trees are cut at different times.

The 'forest lifecycle' is the projected number of years between the tree population becoming established (through regeneration or planting) and being cut down. For the oak trees in the Gâvre forest, this is 130 years.

The 'rotation', as mentioned earlier, is the interval between two cuttings. In a coppice, the rotation period is the same as the forest lifecycle.

An Impostor?

Suddenly I saw **a different kind of chestnut tree**: an old-growth single-trunked tree. **That tree showed what the grove had looked like before it had been coppiced.** It was the only representative of a bygone era. How had it escaped the other trees' fate? Why had it been left there on its own by the path?

I should specify that **all coppiced trees start out as trees with one trunk**. You only have to sow a seed in a pot or on a piece of cotton wool to see that only one stem sprouts from it.

But some species have the interesting characteristic of violently rejecting this plan and allowing other shoots to grow exponentially – much faster than the original trunk. **They have adolescent shoots on a mature stump.**

People have noticed this, and if the wood of those species doesn't have any particular value, they will coppice them. Coppice-based forestry is often preferred. It's fairly simple: the trees are allowed to grow to adulthood, then completely cut down. Very quickly – the following year – shoots grow up around the stump, often near the cambium. So we end up with many trunks instead of just one; of course they're less straight and their growth is less uniform, but there are so many more of them. And they are good enough for garden stakes or firewood.

The Ultimate Break

For a tree, however, the cut is a major trauma. All that is left are the roots and the stump. **Some trees never recover.** Some species just don't have the ability to form shoots.

But other trees cling to life with all their might, like the chestnut trees that were there before me. They had lost their trunks. Oh no, what a disaster! What had they done about it? They had let themselves grieve, then they had given themselves permission

Young shoots on a wise old stump

to live in a totally different way. They had been curious and ventured into the unknown. They had made room for the new parts of themselves to develop.

By allowing new life in, they had found out that they were stronger than before, and they had accepted what they had become: abundant and diverse. Although they never forgot where they came from, and kept their stumps and roots anchored firmly in the earth, they dared to be reborn…

The word 'shoot' glorifies life.

The Past … through a Mirror

Looking at the single-trunked chestnut tree, I saw myself when my parents were still alive and I was first singing on the international stage. Looking at that unique tree, **I felt a sense of solitude … the solitude that followed my dark time, when I lost my voice and my emotions**… an interminable period of solitude, when I refused to leave that false paradise. When I hesitated, **rubbing my palms together, trying to hold on to what had passed away.** When, like a puppeteer, I tried to bring an inanimate body back to life from the inside.

I closed my eyes.

And then I reopened them. I saw the first chestnut tree, then the others around it – those that had been cut and decided to go on living. I could see them clearly before me … multicoloured, vigorous, shining. **Alive**.

And I found the one single-trunked chestnut tree so monotonous, so sad, so different from how I am today.

Oiling the Hinges

Whether a tree loses a bud, a piece of bark or an entire trunk, the **healing always proceeds in the same way**: first mourning, then, while still remaining rooted, unconditional acceptance of the unknown.

What about us? Breaks and ruptures are opportunities, maybe even major opportunities, to access new and welcome parts of ourselves. An undeveloped quality might prove a revelation. When we open the lid of a drab and dusty trunk, we might find treasure. What's more, when these new parts of ourselves emerge, like shoots, we might experience a life force that we were not aware of before. Our energy may grow tenfold.

Whatever else we receive, **the greatest gift will lie in how we live every moment.** As we heal and grow, we may delight in developing our skills, in training ourselves to be present, to listen and to be patient with the rules that we are gradually becoming aware of.

We may take as much pleasure in oiling the hinges and locks on our doors as we do in knowing what's behind each one.

Epilogue: Finally Coming Face to Face with Ourselves

Looking in the mirror, she says, 'Illness, thank you. Thanks to you, I'm completely changing how I look at things. Yes, I'm unstable. Yes, I'm afraid. But thanks to you, I'm finally coming face to face with myself. I'm alive!'

She told me about this on the phone, and a ray of light shone from the speaker. She had just had a cancer-ridden organ removed and she was starting chemotherapy in a few days.

She is so dear to me. I've known her forever.

How about you? Have you ever experienced a major crisis? A major illness? Something that has taken away all your energy, all your zest for life? Something that has made you feel as though you're heading for the land of no return?

Have you ever wondered if you might return, and what you might return to, if you changed completely? If that has happened to you, what choice did you make? Mourning, then rebirth? Or slowly petrifying with eternal regret?

Most importantly, what are you choosing right now? Today? Are you letting young shoots grow out of the stump of your experiences?

EXERCISE

LET YOUR POSSIBILITIES COME TO LIFE

Go to the woods and find a coppiced tree – a tree with multiple trunks, perhaps a chestnut, an oak, a beech or another species.

Greet the tree. Ask if it is ready to welcome you and if it will agree to you doing an exercise with it.

If so, acknowledge it as a survivor, a living being with many lives. In your own way, make physical contact with each of its trunks. Sometimes you can even place your body in between them.

When you are in a stable and balanced position, begin breathing with the tree. Do some INEX+ breathing with it.

Close your eyes.

Are you are living through a major rupture at the moment? Or can you still feel a past break in your heart? Are you still mourning what has gone? Like this tree, have you become strong by letting new possibilities come to life? Whatever your situation, it's time to take inspiration from the tree in your arms.

While continuing your INEX+ breathing, let these four words resonate inside you: *love, sorrow, forgiveness, thanks.* They are inspired by Ho'oponopono, a Hawaiian reconciliation ritual. It can be used both at a time of change and disruption and later, when the memory of it rises up within you.

Repeat these words several times:

~ *Love* ... for myself and every person on this path.

~ *Sorrow* ... for my mistakes and imperfections.

~ *Forgiveness* ... for myself and others ... please.

~ *Thanks* ... gratitude for every life experience.

Do this as many times as you want, both now and in the

future, any time you experience a shock or a break with the past.

Breathe.

Thank the tree.

TIME TO CREATE

🖎 After this experience with the wounded trees, wait until the evening, then sit down and write whatever comes to mind.

~ THE DEEPEST CUT ~

I reject you, I reject myself.
I see you … green shoots within me.
I feel you, green shoots within me.

When I see and feel you,
I allow you to become trunks,
Bundles of light.

Full of life.

WINTER

A Time of Peace

You're beginning to experience life in the present, life in a period of growth and change, and to have an ever-more intimate dialogue with yourself. As you keep reaching for the sky, with your feet and your trunk anchored firmly to the ground, you'll feel that every cell in your body is breathing easily and becoming more peaceful.

During the last three seasons, trees have offered you new tools based on your breath. As you will have found, with practice, INEX+ breathing gets stronger and becomes a reflex. It opens a door to your consciousness and the great space within you. It opens the door to *presence*.

Autumn, with its wounds, its endings and its small and subtle deaths, has offered the perfect chance to learn how to let go. To make peace with the past and thus free yourself in the present.

The leaves are dead now, so they fall to the ground. We don't even hear them leaping into the void. They become birds' wings, floating through the air and then landing – delicately – on the earth.

Fallen leaves no longer belong to a tree. They are once again part of all that is, waves disappearing into the ocean.

They are dead and gone. But the tree lives on … into a time of peace.

TENTH WISDOM

TRANSFORM

We are great transformers. Do you know any living thing that isn't? Can you think of a single moment in your life that hasn't been driven by this fact? We transform in a physiological way: we eat, digest and eliminate. We drink, hydrate ourselves and urinate. Our cells, hair, nails and entire body are constantly being renewed. And that's not even to mention breathing and sleep, through which we regenerate automatically.

Why would our emotions, thoughts and states of mind be any different?

In our attempt to keep our thoughts and feelings in one place, to perhaps lock them in a jewellery box, **we sometimes**

forget – accidentally or on purpose – this principle of renewal. But trees are there to remind us of it. Especially at the end of autumn.

From spring to autumn, trees are active. They transform carbon dioxide and the sugars in their sap, buds and flowers. They produce oxygen, wood, bark, leaves, shoots, fruit and seeds.

Now, all of their leaves are on the ground and a few additional millimetres of sapwood have made their appearance. The living portion of the tree is becoming compost or heartwood.

So we can see that changing what is inside us begins with letting go of everything that has become obsolete, gently saying goodbye to what we digested long ago, to make room for the new. Then the new can find its place and we can live fully and intensely in the present.

As the hours pass, all our heavy and angry emotions become lightness, joy and forgiveness, in the midst of the peaceful feeling that is taking root – forever – within us.

🌿 WINTER, A SEASON OF WONDER 🌿

We honour the season of winter. The winter solstice – the shortest day of the year and the beginning of the return of the light – has been celebrated around the world for millennia. Every tradition has its own term for the solstice: *Dōngzhì* in China, *Yule* for the Celts and the Nordic people, *Sol Invictus* (invincible sun) for the Romans and *Chanukhah* (the Festival of Lights) in the Jewish tradition.

In 354, Pope Liberius chose 25 December as Christ's birthday, calibrating it to the pagan winter solstice celebrations. For the Huron-Wendat nation, that day marks the beginning of the festival period, a time of visiting loved ones and performing healing ceremonies.

In the woods, it seems that foresters and loggers take inspiration from this tradition, for this is the time when they cut trees, create clearings and skid the downed trees. They are right to do this: the cold numbs the trees and weans them from their sap. They are lighter and they dry more quickly. Maybe the anaesthetic of frost numbs what they feel?

In addition, trees are easier to handle when they don't have leaves. It's easier to see their structure then, it's easier to cut their branches and they aren't as affected by the wind.

The remaining trees are also less traumatized. And the machinery moves more easily when the logging roads are frozen. There are fewer ruts and tracks to deal with.

Finally, as the sap begins to flow in the spring, it will help the trees form scars and new shoots.

Winter is definitely the best time for logging.

Lightness

The trees know it. In winter, energy is scarce. That is why they lighten their load.

A learning experience: even in my early thirties, I was still holding on to my secondary school and university textbooks, my clothes from those days, my electric train set and my fireman costume. All of those things were boxed up in my parents' house or my little apartment in Nice, along with a thousand trinkets and papers that reminded me of my carefree childhood – an idealized past.

But nostalgia clings tightly and leaves its mark on the present. One day, I felt as if it was strangling me. There was no choice – I had to sort, sell, give away, throw away... It was as fearsome as it was freeing.

How many tears or angry outbursts had I had over all those objects that were now heading elsewhere? How much pain could I have saved myself if I had disposed of them gradually, over time?

But that's how it was. We need to feel weighed down by our 'stuff' before we get rid of it.

Clearly, this is one of the challenges of being present: becoming so sensitive that healthy renewal happens through micro-digestion, frequently and naturally, without any need to resort to extreme measures. There is no need for a great upheaval because we make micro-adjustments all the time.

It's a gentle transformation.

Life without Winter

If you live in a tropical country, you'll never have experienced autumn, much less winter. For you, the sun rises around 6 a.m.

and sets around 6 p.m., and the 'seasons' consist only of slight variations in humidity: dry season, wet season.

I found this a little disconcerting when I arrived in Burundi. But after a few days I found the lack of variation pleasant and reassuring compared to the many challenges of living in Africa. It was hilarious to experience my first Christmas with a *Pinus patula* and colourful paper garlands when the weather felt like a sauna with mosquitoes. It was 29° Celsius in my house.

Oh, for a breath of cool air… I went searching for one in the forests of the Bugarama or Manga highlands. Up there, in the mountain huts at over 2,000 metres, it wasn't unusual to have a fire in the fireplace. It was so good to relax in front of it after a day of working in the forest with all its deadly black mambas and curious human glances. Everywhere smiling children would be chattering, dignified and secretive men would greet us with a murmur, and strong, brave women would be tilling the soil with their children on their backs.

When I had only just arrived and knew nothing about the tropical forest, I wondered how the trees regenerated. Without winter. Without dropping their leaves. Without rest…

As time passed and I learned more about plant science from my colleagues, I unravelled the mystery. I was astounded to learn that every species was independent: the trees in this red soil of the great African lakes, although certainly affected by the dry season and the rainy season, were much freer than the trees in temperate countries. **Every species chose its own 'winter'.** Their leaves fell at different times of the year.

Those trees teach us a beautiful lesson. **Aren't we all free to choose our time of rest? Our short or long winters**, our pauses, whether for an hour or for a sabbatical year?

Discretion

You don't need to go as far as the tropics to find that freedom. It's there, right there, in our temperate forests. **Some trees just do what they please.** If they decide to defy winter, they just keep their green leaves or needles, even under a blanket of snow.

When other trees look as if they're dead, these evergreens (other than larches, which are deciduous) remain green. They reassure us; they help us stay patient through the bitter months of winter. Their colour leaps out at us through the grey days:

dark green … a lighthouse beacon blazing out across the sea of depression and the ocean of neurosis. These trees are signs of life when all seems dead. They are embryos of warmth around frozen lakes.

And discreetly, without being drawn into the drama of winter, their new needles are coming through. Silently, steadily, moment by moment. The proof lies on the rust-coloured paths running through the forests of spruce, fir and Douglas fir – a thick carpet of needles that cushions the sound of our steps.

Another sweet transition.

Epilogue: Winter as a New Beginning

How do the pages of the book of your life turn? Do you turn them often or do you wait for them to wither away, like parchment covered with old ink: desiccated, heavy and clinging, like limpets clinging to a rock? **What is your pace of change? What is your rhythm of renewal?**

Are there old, stale, out-of-date items stored in your basement or your attic? In your heart or your thoughts? Something from an old aunt or uncle perhaps that you wanted, or even didn't

Silently, fir trees renew themselves

want, but acquired and now daren't get rid of? Are there ideas in your head that you latched on to in childhood and have never dared question? What are those objects hiding? What are those beliefs telling you? In the past, they served a purpose for you or your ancestors. But isn't it time to release them into the world?

Let them hop on a broom and fly away. If you want, just let a few go each year … that's not so bad, is it? Try doing a deep clean every decade: that will open up chasms that will be harder to refill.

And don't forget, all the brilliantly coloured trees are there to hold your hand through this process. They have left behind their old ways, turned red and orange, and then let go of what they have been holding on to. They have released their anger; they have unburdened themselves of the past and all sorts of multicoloured emotions.

EXERCISE

LET GO OF EVERYTHING THAT'S HOLDING YOU BACK

The transformation process begins with casting off old weights that have become obsolete, for example anger or attachments from the past that are dragging you down.

Do this exercise below every time you feel angry or want to detach from a situation or a person.

Go to your usual forest or park. This time, choose a location where you will be at peace.

Stand in the middle of a natural ring of trees. Greet them, then ask if they are willing to welcome you for a few moments. If so, sit cross-legged in the middle of them.

When you are in a stable position, begin breathing with the trees and practise INEX+ breathing (*see page 51*) for a few moments. Settle in and feel your body touching the earth. Feel everything vibrating.

Next, I invite you to explore something different: inhale through your left nostril while closing off your right nostril by pressing down on it with your index finger. Then exhale through your right nostril while closing off your left.

Repeat this five times. Let it feel natural; don't force it. Know that when you exhale through your right nostril, you are getting rid of what is holding you back.

Then do the opposite: inhale through your right nostril, while closing off your left nostril. Exhale through your left nostril, while closing off your right nostril. Repeat this five times. When you exhale through your left nostril, you are getting rid of anger.

To finish the exercise, go back to your INEX+ breathing with both nostrils open. Continue for as long as you wish. Then thank the ring of trees.

TIME TO CREATE

🖎 After this cleansing breathing, calmly and silently put down on paper whatever comes to mind.

~ THE CLEANSING FOREST ~

Trees, with you I dare…
To exhale my silences, so deadened by fossils,
To throw open the suitcases that slumber in my hold,
To wash my clothes that are too small or torn.
And to return everything to the world.

Enjoy Growing Older

Have you ever, at one time or another, encountered a living being that made you look forward to growing old? A living being that had so many positive qualities that you couldn't wait to become more like it? A living being that, without overlooking the negative parts of growing older, was much more emblematic of freedom, inner peace and love of life?

Whether humans, trees or animals, these beings are all around us. What's their secret? They have made the decision to remain fully, intensely alive until their final breath.

Fear of Ageing

Ageing. The very word terrifies us. We shy away from it, or we say 'getting on in years' or 'maturing'. **So many people associate ageing with declining.**

And yes, if we remove ourselves from life, if we stand passively by, waiting for, I don't know, a nudge towards the fountain of youth, it might feel as if we're gradually losing our capacities. And that's true. We do lose our physical abilities, our mental acuity, our resilience and our vitality as time goes by. Even if we take good care of our body, it will get weaker, break down and wither over time.

But what if we had a different mindset about the passing of time? What if we could allow precious stones to emerge from the sea foam in our heart?

With age comes wisdom, knowledge and the ability to love and to give back to others. Death nourishes life. Not only our final death, but all the little deaths that disrupt our path through life, just as the slow rotting of a tree trunk creates nesting places for owls and holes for ants and bees, and the gentle rotting of leaves creates compost for moss, ivy and lichen, and humus for new trees. This is the joy of giving back, the joy of passing something on, and it wells up spontaneously.

If, in our immaturity, we stay in the mode of receiving, consuming, fiercely attached to our youth, over time we feel ourselves becoming diminished ... inexorably. But **if we switch our mindset to loving, giving and sharing, we will grow**, steadily, until we reach the end of the path.

Enriching others until the end of our existence – this is the only treasure that will go with us to the other side.

The Wise Woman Emmanuelle

Maybe ageing is simpler for fir trees. Because **a fir tree's finest hour is the second half of its life.** It has no – or few – regrets about the past, unlike sun-loving trees, which see their best days as being behind them as the years go by.

Some people are exactly like great firs. I experienced this for myself in 1998 through a chance encounter on a railway platform in Nice. That day, **the renowned social activist Sister Emmanuelle assured me that her life, her true life, had begun when she was around**

*A wise old being
that gives new life*

60 years old and decided to leave the safe nest of her convent in France to climb the rubbish heaps of Cairo. There, among the poor, she saw beacons of humanity in the midst of the city's crime, vermin and crushing pain. And there came a time when she no longer envied those in 'developed' countries who seemed to have everything while their poor shrivelled hearts were groaning inside.

On that railway platform, her joy was seared into the bark of the spoiled, depressed young man that I was then. Her words were imprinted forever on my pulp.

Daily nourishment, hand on heart, head bowed.

✖ THE WORLD'S MEMORIES ✖

Trees hold the world's memories. Some can live up to 5,000 years, like the bristlecone pine (*Pinus longaeva*) in the mountains of California. In 2017, one was thought to be 5,066 years old.

France's oldest tree is an olive tree (*Olea europaea*) in Roquebrune-Cap-Martin that is about 2,000 years old.

But if we include trees that reproduce through cloning, the oldest are far, far older. There is a 10,000-year-old spruce (*Picea abies*) living in Sweden and an 80,000-year-old colony of quaking aspen (*Populus tremuloides*) in Utah, in the United States. On a human scale, the length of these lives is unimaginable.

We can determine a tree's age using a technique called dendrochronology. A Pressler auger is used to take a core sample from the trunk, about one metre from the ground. If that sample reaches the heart of the tree, then the number of rings can be counted and the age established.

Elephant on the Erdre

It's an immense living being, and not only in terms of size. Once I'd got over my amazement at its diameter – some three metres – and the feeling of being dwarfed by its crown of leaves, I learned, thanks to an explanatory plaque, that this chestnut tree is truly one of our planetary ancestors. It is 1,200 years old. It met Charlemagne. It is one of the oldest trees in France. It lives by the Erdre river in the heart of Nantes. I bow to it!

I often sit watching it. As with most old beings, its highest points have withered. Its 10-tonne branches are now supported by wooden crutches that people have put there. Without them, the branches would already have cracked, fallen to the ground and rotted. It is covered in blisters. Here and there, its trunk is dotted with rotten spots, places that are half dead. It is a forest unto itself. Its trunk forms a valiant spiral and seems to pierce both earth and sky, while its branches spread to form a fertile breeding-ground, giving rise to other branches that look like bonsai trees in silhouette: straight and bursting with life. But its bark isn't strong enough to conceal everything. There are large swathes of dead wood there, looking like stripped planks.

At the level of its stump, new shoots, leaves and suckers haughtily rise up from its wounds, which seem to sink almost to its roots. These tender green shoots look like hot-headed teenagers, clinging to their wise old stump.

Youth knows where to learn. Age passes its joy along. Young and old co-exist. In one living being.

Don't forget, even if your trunk gives away your age, that what you are living now is youth, endlessly renewed.

Standing there like an old elephant on the way to the graveyard, this tree is everything at once: trunk, shoots, rot, the intensity of verdant life. **It is an incarnation of reincarnation on the scale of one life; it is the experience of resurrection repeated every moment.**

It exemplifies resilience.

That is how I want to grow old: enriched by 1,200 harvests, by 1,200 winters, by the healing of 1,200 wounds. So many, and so multicoloured.

Dialogue

'I love it when you come and see me.'

'Huh? What?'

'I said, "I love it when you come and see me."'

I'm looking round, trying to see who's talking to me. There's no one there. I was born in Lorraine, where Joan of Arc came from, so I'm not surprised by occasionally hearing voices. But now there's silence. I think about something else and continue observing the large chestnut tree.

'I love you and I'm happy to see you again...'

There it is again — a voice, but not a voice. Words, but not words. A feeling disguised as words so that I can understand. My heart trembles.

'But ... who's talking to me?'

'I am, love. I'm here, in front of you.'

'Oh, you! Hiding behind the chestnut tree. Come out!'

'I'm *here*, in front of you. Open the eyes of your heart. My heart is open wide for you.'

'What? That's you? The chestnut tree?'

'At last! I love it when you come and see me.'

I didn't understand this with my head. I only understood that an ocean was welling out of my heart, out of my eyes and down my cheeks.

'Feel all of this love and tell them who we are — the old trees, with our wounds and our pock marks, supported by crutches.

We are love.'

After that there were no more words, despite my fervent questions.

I left that spot by the Erdre wondering if I'd been dreaming. All I knew was that my heart would remain bathed in a love that was constant, abundant and peaceful.

Dream or no dream, that was what the tree gave to me.

'Love': the Trees' Word

Some say that they 'communicate' with trees and with their energies. Others maintain that trees talk to us. And others, like me, perceive a great deal when they are physically with trees, without really knowing what to call it. I'm not looking for anything more. **I savour what I receive in the presence of the chestnut, the beech, the oak and Doug.**

That night, as I was falling asleep, words hopped, skipped and danced in my mind.

'The voice of the wise old chestnut tree is your voice…'

Epilogue: The Wellspring of Life

Are you happy to go out and meet elders? If you are already an elder yourself, how do you perceive your existence? Are you aware of the priceless treasure that is revealed as you age?

Of course, you probably haven't succeeded at everything you've wanted to and the world you're getting ready to leave behind is undoubtedly imperfect, but that's the reality of the limitations of human life.

But there is still so much that you can pass on. Who hasn't been moved by the glow that passes between a grandparent and their grandchildren or great-grandchildren?

All of this happens at the gates to the 'wellspring of life', from which some have just arrived and to which others will soon return.

Some of us, in the West, 'park' our elders in homes away from the eyes of the world. Others honour them, consult them, listen to their words, care for them until their final breath. They understand that elders are sources of wisdom and inspiration.

When you look at old trees, aren't you impressed by their grandeur, their roots, their branches and their thickness? By their resilience, by their unique experiences, all of which are on display right before your eyes?

Why wouldn't we feel this way when we look at our own ancestors?

EXERCISE

LET YOURSELF BE FILLED WITH LIGHT

Choose a special moment and go and look for a very old tree, the largest and oldest that you can find. It's there now, waiting for you.

Greet the tree and ask if it welcomes you. If it gives a resounding 'Yes!', open your arms wide and spread your entire body around its trunk.

After a few moments, turn round and stand or sit with your back pressed against the tree. In that position, begin your INEX+ breathing (*see page 51*).

As you're breathing, feel a ray of white light entering the crown of your head. Let the feeling grow.

Let this light fill you a little more each time you exhale. Little by little, let it fill your head, then your neck, then your shoulders, lungs, heart and so on, right down to your feet.

You are now full of light, with your back pressed against a 100-year-old tree. Breathe. Feel that light in your entire being, in your entire history.

Remain there as long as you like, then thank the tree with all your heart.

TIME TO CREATE

➤ Do you feel more alive and vibrant after this light-filled breathing? Write down what it brings up for you.

~ WHERE AM I GOING? ~

I am going to die.

I am almost a year old and I know it.

I am 10 years old and I have forgotten it.

I am 18 years old and I couldn't care less about it.

I am 40 years old and I am aware of it.

I am 60 years old and I am consumed by it.

I am 80 years old and I am right there.

Ready.

REST

It is the heart of winter and everything has slowed down. The trees have shed their final drops of life; their leaves are on the ground and their sap is barely flowing. The danger is frost. But a few beech trees are doing their best to keep roses in their cheeks. As long as it's not windy, their copper-tinted leaves will still be there, clinging to their branches.

Larch, on the other hand, thinks it's a deciduous tree: it drops its yellowed needles all in one go. The other conifers take on a heavy responsibility – to be green beacons in a world that is gradually joining a dance in black and white. **Mother Nature is all-powerful, and she always has the last word.** Once she decides that black and white is the mood of the moment, she adorns her beacons – and the sleeping world – with a blanket of white cotton wool. Everything is muffled. Tucked in. Life is all one, and it invites us to the great sleep.

Pauses, Long and Short

Do you allow yourself to go along with winter? Whether it's a season, a day or a life? Do you listen to your inner voice when it orders you to take a few minutes, or a few days, of well-deserved rest?

I don't always do this, and sometimes I pay dearly for it. Very recently, in 2017, I was trapped in a whirlwind of doing too much, wanting to do everything, and life knocked me down. I ended up in hospital. With a charming illness, wrapped up in a bow, like a present under the Christmas tree. Too little sleep, too much sap expended on my emotions, too little contact with my inner self and not enough time with my brothers, the trees... A mess.

I had forgotten the second wisdom. I had fallen headlong into the trap of being overworked, and had to learn, yet again, that trees are priceless as brothers. I had barely returned to their domain – silently, alone – when my fatigue disappeared just like that.

Making mistakes. Learning. Always learning.

Having respect for the right tempo and staying in contact with ourselves are part of everyday life. Doug, help me never forget this again.

Winter, at the Source

In winter, wherever I am in the world, I return to my source, the Moyeuvre forest or the Vosges forest, home to my first breaths, my first laughter. **The people who held out their hands to me then are no longer there, but the trees are.** The trees are still there.

I see them stripped bare now, naked, asleep. I see that they know exactly what to do.

I feel that they welcome this brutal season of winter with the same grace with which they greet the first breaths of spring. I feel them staying calm at all times.

I touch them and they teach me.

No tree makes a decision to keep producing leaves, buds or seeds in the depths of winter. That would be suicidal.

So why do we do that?

One Life, Many Sons

In the Dabo forest, I stand and breathe in front of the mountain ash under which my childhood pet dog is buried. I breathe in front of the Scots pines that cling to the rock covered with raspberry canes where I proudly climbed in my grandfather's footsteps, my mouth crammed with blueberries. I breathe under the bare branches of the cherry tree I found on my very first fruit-picking expedition. Near the rabbits that are here with me, I smell the sweet winter scent of the pine trees. I know each one of them. There's the one who dried my tears with his moss handkerchief!

In Moyeuvre-Petite, I go to the spot where the big tree grew in front of our house. There's no trace of him left now, just pavement. **But I remember him: a giant spruce. He visited me in my dreams. He was home to 100 blue tits.** I loved him. He stood alone, but he joyfully invited me to go and meet his brothers in the great forest.

So I went to play up on the hill with the fossils, or on the slag heap of tailings from the Lorraine mines. It was a miserable piece of land where few pioneers dared try their luck. But there were pioneers there: they were called birches, and they were so happy with so little.

Today, the tailings heap is gone. The last I heard was that it was my childhood best friend, now a big-shot business owner, who took the stones and dust from it to pave roads. Maybe it was that asphalt that covered my spruce tree's stump. Does that tree know that for a long time I kept the permit that authorized his removal?

The slag heap has gone and the earth is bare now. But not quite. **Tiny trees are growing; some are already tall enough to poke through the snow.**

Intimacy

I'm resting. There's nothing I have to do today. Under the canopy of my Vosges trees, everything feels rich. I'm idling along a forest path dotted with stones that are massaging the soles of my feet. I'm feeling deeply connected to the sweet intimacy of my own presence. A few metres further on, under a stand of evergreen trees, the path is carpeted, hospitably, with pine needles and moss. I take off my shoes and keep walking, stretching my feet with each step.

Later, it looks like rain. I am thrilled with the abundant, free, generous, life-giving rain. Up higher, when the rain turns to snow and the west wind blasts the ridges, I like to seal myself up in a modest protective lair.

As I walk home, I realize that nothing is solely good or bad. Sun, rain and snow are all precious in the right proportions. It is when there is an excess of one or another of them that they can be deadly.

🌿 FOREST BATHING 🌿

This practice flourished in the 1980s and was bolstered by scientific endorsements in the mid-1990s. In 1995, a team of researchers demonstrated that walking in the woods significantly reduced five psychological problems: tension, anxiety, depression, fatigue and confusion. Later, an analysis of the subjects' saliva cortisol levels showed that the forest had a significant stress-relieving effect. Other tests have shown that a 'forest bath' reduces blood sugar levels in people with diabetes and increases immunity in general. It also improves mood.

How can we explain this? Some might point to the trees' essential oils. For example, smelling the scent of the Japanese cedar for one minute rapidly lowers systolic blood pressure.

Being in the forest, away from screens and phones, also encourages us to get in touch with our senses. A 'forest bath' allows us to reconnect to nature. And our body will thank us for it.

Intense Flavours

Descending from Hohneck, **I am intensely present. And even when I'm not, I'm aware that I'm not. And I change that.** It's a delicious ongoing give-and-take. I have fun with it.

All the Douglas fir greeted me just now. I took some of them in my arms. Earlier, I felt the maple syrup coursing through the maples' hearts. So many gifts. Such a balm for the soul. So much beauty on every branch.

Lower down, a small white butterfly lands on a tree's powerful bark. Do you know, tree, that I saw that butterfly, fragile, tiny and motionless on your giant trunk, as you cradled him gently?

A few hundred metres lower down, my eyes rest on you, baby Douglas fir, even though you are not a metre tall. And right away I notice your wound: your highest branch, bare, dead and suffocating the others. I don't try to understand why; I just take out my pocket knife and cut it off. The other branches have to be able to breathe, to take over.

As I stand there caressing you, little Doug, just after freeing you, a miracle occurs. Ten metres away, a young deer bursts out of the woods and pauses on the path to get his bearings. He looks around him, his head crowned with a large rack of antlers, the virile indication of a young male. His body is in profile, his head facing me. His nostrils tremble. And then he is off, moving slowly, almost peacefully, out of my sight, away from my human scent.

A rare sighting in the Vosges in the middle of the day. Thank you for that, Doug.

My Journey Goes On

Another rest day. This time in the Parc du Charmois in Vandoeuvre-lès-Nancy.

At first, I was attracted to an ash tree leaning over a great expanse of green lawn, but then I decided to go to what I assumed was a maple tree. My head chose the maple because of my love for Quebec, but my heart had initially guided me to the ash.

I went to the maple and sat down at its foot. But I couldn't get comfortable and I got impatient. Then I looked up and noticed that the trunk I was leaning against belonged to a young ash that was so engulfed by the three maple trees around it that it was entirely hidden.

That was it: I went over and sat down at the foot of the first ash that had called to me. I greeted it and asked if it was willing to welcome me. My tree friend for that day would be that ash after all.

And I felt good. I felt that the tree had said yes. A wonderful yes.

I lay on my belly, my head against the ash's trunk, and breathed. First of all, I felt the crown of my head in very strong contact with the tree, as if I were a ram headbutting it. I played with my ash, gently turning my head to make contact with it with a larger part of my skull. The bark was a delicately scented greyish-orange pastel colour and felt soft. And then, all of a sudden, without losing that voluptuous feeling in the crown of my head, I became aware of my shoulders, my thorax, my stomach, the tops of my thighs, my knees and the tops of my feet – they were all one, in contact with the earth.

With every out-breath, I felt my body settling into the earth. Everything was good. The ash was there at my head, massaging my hairy armour, calming my mind, tempering my thoughts. Emboldened by this full-body experience, I sensed that I could safely go further. And I did. My entire body started vibrating. Sometimes it was hot, sometimes cold, with pricking sensations here and tickling sensations there. And with every breath, every layer of my body, from my skin down to my bone barrow, moved like a wave. Every cell was in motion and I even felt that the beautiful ash tree was moving with me.

Sometimes I hear voices in my head, singing softly, 'I feel good. Everything's fine. I'm present. I have to concentrate, so I don't lose it.' And just at that moment when I'm trying to stop time, to hold that presence, I lose my connection to what is. All of a sudden, my nose pressed into the earth and the grass, I say, 'Hello, thought! Welcome!' The thought feels acknowledged, so it fades away. And I come back to myself.

This time, without overthinking, instead I breathed audibly. The sound of my voice took over from the silence but accompanied the silence. It accompanied all the movement. It accompanied the life. It remained fragile between two great sighs, then asserted itself: full, vibrant, as shiny and round as a copper kettledrum.

Who knows how long that went on for? It was a slice of winter in my day, a rest amid the absolute joy of feeling alive.

Trees, Trees, Everywhere

Everything I felt then is still with me now. I realize I can tap into that state of presence whenever I want. I can stay connected to my tree, to my trees, at the bottom of a mine, or in the concrete jungle of a city, or in my office, on the underground or in my car. Trees, my brothers, you are always there in my heart. I can feel your presence even when I'm far away from you. I can feel connected to all of you. You are all, every one of you, residents of the Earth.

This gives me strength. Nothing scares me. I'm alive, with you, and I can relax into the life that is unfolding for me.

Trees, with you, I am free. We are all free.

Trees are with me everywhere

EXERCISE

THANK THE WORLD'S TREES

You too ... you are free.

And you have been given 12 wisdoms. Some will have resonated with you more than others. Using those as a basis, choose the ones that are the most appropriate for the current situations in your life and apply them. You can even create your own exercises if you wish.

You know now how to meet a tree, or a grove, or even a whole forest. You know that whether trees are right there in front of you or in your cellular memory, they are with you now.

Greet them. Ask if they welcome you.

When you get a resounding 'Yes!', make physical contact, using your skin or your memory. You choose how and when.

Begin INEX+ breathing (*see page 51*).

Now I invite you to go further. Use all of your flesh that touches the outside world to touch the earth, or the bark of a tree.

Now it's time to clear out your body from the inside. Feel it pulsating as energy leaves you; feel it pulsating where your skin is touching the earth, or the bark of a tree.

Then, deeper down, feel it slowly filling back up.

Take your time. Continue for as long as you like.

Then thank the trees with all of your heart. Thank the trees that have supported you since you started reading this book, since you began this great journey through their wisdoms.

And thank the others. Thank every forest in the world.

Protect them. Love them. Love them all.

TIME TO CREATE

✍ Completely freely, and with all of your love, set some words down on paper, which is of course made of trees. Their ultimate gift is offering up their material for our words to dance on. Let them share themselves with you now.

The important thing is not what you write, but how you perceive the act of writing. Movement, sound, colour, the scent of the ink and the paper, the pressure of your fingers on the pen or pencil, the contrast between your warm fingers and the cooler feeling of the pen or pencil, the distance between your eyes and the paper...

What is vibrating, pulsating or whirling within you now? Where? How? Do you feel grounded? Are the sensations changing as the seconds are passing? How about your thoughts? What melodies are swirling through your mind?

Savour everything. Savour it all.

BE

Tree. You are but a moment, in harmony. You connect us to the mystery of our existence, whether we're atheist or religious, practising or not. Some call this sacred, others simply call it life, and others call it the background to our lives.

Trees, many traditions speak of you as precious living beings that accompany us on the road to our destiny. And you are everywhere. With Christ on the Mount of Olives; in sacred Native American groves. You are the oaks of the Celts and the Greeks, the sacred fig in India, which has been worshipped since Buddha's time, the olive trees in the Koran, the Jewish tradition's boxthorn, the silver birch that is sacred to the Nordic peoples. And scripture cites so many other examples…

While religions and other traditions differentiate themselves through words and practices that are sometimes at odds, you accompany us throughout life quite naturally, without exception, and nothing about you goes against our beliefs. Whatever those beliefs, we have seen you, touched you, tasted you, felt you, listened to you. You invite us to breathe consciously. Your wooden heart is the door to the great beings that we are – beings whose inner lives extend far beyond what we see in the physical world.

It's up to us to push that door open.

Then there is nothing more to do but let go, let things happen and go confidently with nature's flow.

This doesn't mean remaining passive – just the opposite. Each and every day, we cultivate an intense spirit of presence. As you do. But we no longer act on our emotional impulses or desires; we simply let our dreams and desires come to life.

Life, ecstatic to see us returning, then rolls out the red carpet for us and gives our desires and dreams the best chance of coming true. And if they don't do so immediately, by knowing how to acknowledge, and thus soften, our attachments and expectations, we can turn the situation into an opportunity.

Walking this path in the company of trees will, I hope, have offered you an array of tools to discover and nourish your deepest self. In that space, where we feel vibrant, where we breathe, rooted in all that supports us, we welcome the insights and emotions that flow through us without ever thinking that we are them or letting ourselves drown in their ferocious power.

Because this space is so vast, there is room for everything that lives within us and through us. A river may flow into an ancient flood plain. An ocean may calmly absorb its own fury in an estuary.

We experience this space not through the filter of our mind or spirit, but through feeling everything that happens without effort in our lives. Through INEX+. That has a particular feel to it. And it's in perpetual motion.

As we continue down this path, we become more and more aware. We love everything about ourselves, and we no longer say, 'I'm sick,' 'I'm afraid,' 'I'm in pain,' or 'I'm sad.' Instead we say, 'A part of me is sick,' 'Fear is rising up within me,' 'Pain is rising up within me,' or 'The sad part of me has been activated.' And that makes all the difference.

When a thought comes up, we are able to say, 'Hello, thought,' and then no longer identify with that thought. We let it be, and it passes, and it fades.

Tree. You know who you are. You know that you are both a single unique tree and the sum of all the forests in the world. In that vastness, you watch yourself living. You are a living witness to the mystery, and you never forget it. We humans are sometimes distracted. You remind us who we are.

Let's prepare the land, plant the seed and water it every day. Then let's allow the tree to grow.

With you, Doug, and with your siblings all over the world. Forever.

Acknowledgements

First of all, thank you to the trees. I've already expressed my gratitude to them on every page of this book, but I can never express it enough.

Next, with all my heart, I thank the beings of light who have illuminated my wanderings through the woods from my earliest years to the present day:

My father, **Philippe Karche**, for all the hours spent picking mushrooms in the forest.

My grandfather **Paul Karche**, my hero during my time in the Vosges forests.

My godmother, **Claude Meyer**, for funding my forestry studies and typing my Canadian internship report before computers existed.

My friends **Frédéric Chédot**, **Bruno Pasturel**, **Jean-Michel D'Orazio**, **Jean-Yves Magot**, **Fabrice Dercq** and all of the students in the 19th graduating class of the BTS in forestry programme at the Poisy-Annecy agricultural school (1987–1989). All of them still work in forestry as of 2017.

I also thank my professors from that programme.

Guy Laflamme, the forestry engineer who oversaw the student exchange programme at the CEGEP in Rimouski, Quebec, in 1988.

Martin Lemieux, my dear and thoughtful colleague from the Ministry of Recreation, Fish, and Game in Sherbrooke, Quebec (1988).

Alain Lussier, another Ministry colleague who opened doors for me on Anticosti Island in 1988.

Luc Jochem, a surveyor with the land office in Metz in 1989, who helped polish my application to the VSNA (National Active Service Volunteer) programme in Burundi.

Jean-Marie Rausch, the mayor and minister of Metz, who supported my application to the VSNA in Burundi in 1989.

Hervé Duchaufour, project director at the ISABU (Burundi Graduate School of Agronomy) in 1990.

Onesphore Bitoki, **Hippolyte Ndikumwami**, **Melchior Bizimana**, **Augustin Gahungu** and **Dahlia Nijimbere**, dear colleagues at the ISABU in 1990–1991. **Melchior Bizimana**, who perished in the Burundian genocide in 1993, has a special place in my heart.

Pierre Poupard, director of the Bujumbura *chorale* in 1990, who was one of the first people to identify my potential as a tenor.

Jean-Marie Pennes, a French forestry engineer with the VSNA in Burundi in 1991. Colleague, friend, brother, I will never forget you.

Jacky Bedos, my colleague at the Languedoc-Roussillion CRPF in Carcassonne in 1992–1993.

Sister Emmanuelle, a bright light in the world. Thank you for loving me unconditionally for 20 minutes in 1998.

With the blessing of **Régent Garihwa Sioui**, chief of the Huron-Wendat First Nation, who welcomed me to Tsonontwan (Quebec) nature and culture site in 2006. Also thanks to **Rémi**.

Helen Roy, a friend in Quebec whom I met in Tsonontwan in 2006 and who hosts mindfulness events in nature.

Denis Haberkorn, director of the Voix Alsace project, who supported me in creating RandOlyric in the Munster valley in 2010.

Olivier Claude, director of the Ballons des Vosges regional nature park, who welcomed the RandOlyric project in 2010. Thanks also to **Violaine Pautot**.

To RandOlyric's partners: **André Sidre** and the hosts of Vosges en Marche; **Dominique Schoenheitz** and **Francine Klur**, vineyard owners in Wihr-au-Val and Katzenthal; **Gilles Péquigniot**, the musician who makes the trees sing.

Salah Benzacour, the organizer of the 2012 TedX Alsace events, who gave me the opportunity to speak there and share my story of finding resilience in the First Nations' forests in Quebec.

Grégoire Legendre, director of the Opéra de Québec, the first opera festival to include RandOlyric in its offerings, in 2013.

Guy Lessard, the only other tenor/forestry technician I know. I'm so glad to have found you, Guy; I feel less alone!

The teachers at the Kopan Buddhist centre in Kathmandu, Nepal, for all of the life-giving breaths I experienced there in 2014.

Thank you to all the people who went on RandOlyric walks between 2010 and 2019: more than 2,000 of you, aged six months to 85 years.

Huge thanks to the therapists who have opened my mind and my eyes throughout my life.

Florence Lautrédou, author of numerous books, who has a wonderful talent for bringing the right people together at the right time. Most of all, thank you for your friendship!

Odile Dujardin, who allowed us to host the final RandOlyric walk in Le Gâvre on her inspiring property, La Parenthèse guest house in Saint-Omer-de-Blain, in 2017.

Jean-Paul Leroux, president of the Maison de la Forêt du Gâvre (44), who poured his passion into introducing me to that forest in 2017.

Olivier Deparday, the director who magnificently filmed *Les voix de la forêt* (Voices of the Forest)[24] for RandOlyric in 2017.

Pascale Senk, for connecting me to Les Éditions Leduc.s, and for his invaluable advice on publishing this book.

Crocus the rabbit, who has accompanied me on my travels recently.

Thank you to my French publisher, Les Éditions Leduc.s, who helped to bring this book to life. Special thanks to **Liza Faja**, **Claire Nicolet**, for the incredible drawings, and **Élisabeth Boyer**. Your straightforward feedback improved the book, and your comments were full of care, enthusiasm and respect. That is a rare and precious thing.

Finally, thank you to **Corinne McKay** for the inspired English translation, and a heartfelt thank you to **Hay House UK** for sharing *Tree Wisdom* around the English-speaking world.

The adventure among the trees continues, with new RandOlyric events and meditative forest walks. For more information, visit my website: www.randolyric.com.

----

24 You can view this video at www.deparday.fr and www.randolyric.com.

ABOUT THE AUTHOR

Vincent Karche is an author, forester, opera tenor and TedX speaker. Born near the majestic Moyeuvre forest in France, he enjoyed a career as a celebrated opera singer but was struck speechless after a severe burnout.

Only after a four-month immersion experience in the forests of Quebec was Vincent able to rediscover his voice, his true self and his mission in life: to help others reconnect with the healing power of trees.

He now leads RandOlyrics retreats, which marry singing and forest bathing, in the Gâvre Forest in France, and also delights audiences at the Angers Nantes Opera.

www.randolyric.com

Hay House Podcasts
Bring Fresh, Free Inspiration Each Week!

Hay House proudly offers a selection of life-changing audio content via our most popular podcasts!

Hay House Meditations Podcast

Features your favorite Hay House authors guiding you through meditations designed to help you relax and rejuvenate. Take their words into your soul and cruise through the week!

Dr. Wayne W. Dyer Podcast

Discover the timeless wisdom of Dr. Wayne W. Dyer, world-renowned spiritual teacher and affectionately known as "the father of motivation." Each week brings some of the best selections from the 10-year span of Dr. Dyer's talk show on Hay House Radio.

Hay House Podcast

Enjoy a selection of insightful and inspiring lectures from Hay House Live events, listen to some of the best moments from previous Hay House Radio episodes, and tune in for exclusive interviews and behind-the-scenes audio segments featuring leading experts in the fields of alternative health, self-development, intuitive medicine, success, and more! Get motivated to live your best life possible by subscribing to the free Hay House Podcast.

Find Hay House podcasts on iTunes, or visit www.HayHouse.com/podcasts for more info.

HAY HOUSE

Look within

Join the conversation about latest products,
events, exclusive offers and more.

 Hay House UK

 @HayHouseUK

 @hayhouseuk

 healyourlife.com

We'd love to hear from you!